# QUEST

This book won second prize in The Scripture Union competition for new writers.

First published 1985

ISBN 0 86201 302 X



Printed and bound in Great Britain by Cox & Wyman Ltd., Reading

# The KING'S QUEST

**Lynette Bishop**

SCRIPTURE UNION
130 City Road, London EC1V 2NJ

# 1

It began one day at breakfast. Simon and Jenny laughed and chattered as they thought of the long, lazy weeks of the summer holidays stretching ahead of them. They always loved coming on holiday to the conservation zone. There was nowhere else quite like it. It had been specially created to reproduce the most attractive features of Earth back in the twentieth century.

'Can you believe those old cars!' commented Simon.

'Can you believe these cornflakes?' added Jenny, laughing. 'You've been eating them as if you won't get any food till the next holidays!'

Jenny was so excited she hardly touched her food. A mysterious visitor with a strange name was coming to share their holiday. She was arriving that very afternoon. Simon managed to wolf down a second slice of toast as Jenny chattered on.

'I wonder what she'll look like. Mum, do you know what she looks like?'

'No. I just know she's a bit older than you. Finish your cornflakes, Jenny. I've got a lot to do.' Mrs Miller began picking up some empty bowls and cups. 'Your father's left half his tea again,' she sighed.

'Poor Dad having to work while we're on holiday,' commented Simon through a mouthful of toast.

His mother paused. 'Yes, it's a shame,' she said. 'But at least he can get to the Defence Plant quite quickly from here.'

'Yeah. He gets to drive in a car every day!' enthused Simon.

'Only as far as the border of the conservation zone,' amended his mother, smiling. 'Perhaps you could have a ride with him one morning.'

'It would be nicer if things eased off at work and Daddy could join us,' said Jenny.

Her mother frowned down at the dishes in her hands. 'We'll just have to wait and see,' she said and turned quickly into the kitchen.

Jenny had noticed in the past few weeks how worried her father had looked when he came home from work. He had tried to smile and joke as he usually did, teasing Simon about the amount of food he ate and Jenny about her chattering, but he looked tired and a far-away look would come into his eyes as if he was puzzling over something difficult and sad. It had not really been a surprise when he had told them he would have to commute to work, for the first week or so of their holiday at least.

Jenny chattered on about the visitor. 'I hope she won't mind sharing a room with me.'

'I'll have to tell her there's an empty rabbit hutch at the bottom of the garden,' teased Simon. 'It might make a welcome change after the first night.'

'Oh you!' Jenny pulled a face at him and looked round for something to throw at him.

The doorbell rang. 'Phew, saved by the bell,' breathed Simon. Jenny jumped up from her seat and knocked the marmalade over. 'It's her!'

'Can't be,' said Simon. 'It's too early.'

'Oh no,' muttered their mother, wiping her hands on a towel as she rushed to the door.

But it was not the visitor after all. It was only Mrs Jeavons, a rather gossipy lady from the house two doors away. Simon and Jenny heard her quavering voice in the hall.

'I do hope you don't mind my calling, Mrs Miller, but I thought if anyone knew if it was true, it would be you. Is there . . . has there . . .?' and here she lowered her voice so that Jenny and Simon could not make out what she said. But they heard clearly enough their mother's startled response: 'An invasion!'

Mrs Jeavons sounded relieved. 'Then it's not true. I'm so glad. Someone said that some Gehallen spaceships had been seen quite near the city. I know they've talked of the possibility of an attack for years, but . . . It's not true then? I thought with Mr Miller working at the Defence Plant, you . . .'

'Mrs Jeavons,' came their mother's voice, sounding quite firm as it did when she told them it really *was* bed-time. 'I'm sure my husband would have been one of the first to know if an invasion was at all likely.'

'Yes, of course.' Mrs Jeavons sounded apologetic. 'I'm sorry to have worried you.'

Their mother's voice softened. 'That's quite all right. Don't you worry now. Everything's fine.'

Simon and Jenny slid quickly back into their seats as they heard the front door click shut.

'Can you clear the breakfast things for me, please?' Their mother looked round the door. 'I'm just going to phone Daddy.'

But she didn't, because the doorbell rang again. This time it was a man's voice, deep with a hint of laughter in it.

'I'm sorry we're so early,' he was saying, as he walked into the room. He was quite tall, but there was nothing very special about him; yet when he stepped into the room Simon and Jenny forgot about everything else except him.

'Simon and Jenny,' he said, smiling at them. 'I'm Michael. I'm very pleased to meet you both.' And from the warmth in his brown eyes, they felt he really meant it. 'I'm sure Andromeda will feel very much at home here.'

Andromeda, the visitor. So she was here at last. They

looked past him to the slender girl with fair hair falling softly to her shoulders. She walked forward, holding out her hand and they felt the same warmth from her friendly smile and dark eyes.

'Hello Jenny, Simon,' she said. Jenny, for perhaps the first time in her life was completely lost for words.

'Nice to meet you ... Andromeda,' said Simon awkwardly.

'It's lovely to have you,' added his mother warmly. 'We hope you'll be very much at home with us.' Simon was pleased to see that she too was smiling and relaxed. All the earlier worries seemed to have gone. She didn't even mind the uncleared table with their half-eaten breakfast on it, now.

But none of them knew, at that moment, that Andromeda would not be settling happily into their home. None of them could possibly have guessed what lay ahead. Simon and Jenny would certainly have finished up their breakfast if they had known it was to be their last proper meal for days.

Jenny had found her tongue and was chatting to Andromeda. Simon was listening to Michael talking to his mother. She did not usually talk freely with strangers, so Simon was surprised to hear her talk of Mrs Jeavons' visit and the rumour of an invasion. Simon was to remember Michael's reply later because it was so strange. He had not said 'Don't worry' or, 'Isn't that silly.' He had said, 'We must always remember, whatever happens, that the King has put power over everything in the hands of the Prince.'

Simon was about to ask him what he meant, when something happened which made them all stop talking and turn to the breakfast table. It was a 'Miaow.' Sitting at the foot of the table was a black and brown cat hopefully eyeing a spilt cup of milk.

'Oh, Alabaster!' exclaimed Andromeda, laughing. 'It's not polite to beg when you haven't even been introduced.

This is my furry and greedy friend Alabaster. I didn't know how you would feel about him staying, Mrs Miller? Michael can easily take him back when he goes.'

Jenny and Simon looked hopefully at their mother. She looked at the appealing bundle of fur. 'Alabaster, you're very welcome,' said Mrs Miller, tipping the rest of the cup of milk into the saucer. 'But I thought alabaster was a white stone? He's black and brown from head to toe.'

Andromeda smiled. 'He's a very unusual cat,' she said.

Even when Michael left, the happy, relaxed atmosphere stayed. Their mother was not even worried when she couldn't reach their father on the video-phone. So they were quite calm and collected when the strange noises in the street began. It was only when Mrs Miller looked out of the window that her face became tense. She turned to Andromeda and said quietly, 'It's the Grey Gunners.'

So Mrs Jeavons had been right after all; for the Grey Gunners were the deadly and merciless secret army of the planet Gehalla. The rulers of Gehalla and the leaders of their regular army said that all they wanted was peace and denied that the Grey Gunners existed. But rumours of their cruel attacks on other planets had reached Earth. Everyone knew about the Grey Gunners; the awful things they did, the terrifying way they looked. But no one had really believed they would ever dare invade Earth.

Simon's eyes widened. 'An invasion!'

'We must get quickly to the secret shelter,' said Mrs Miller. 'Come on! Hurry!'

Simon was the first to slip into the small room, built behind a false fireplace. Andromeda followed with Alabaster and finally Jenny. It was not until their mother slid the panel shut that they realised she was not coming. Jenny made a move to open the panel.

'No,' said Andromeda gently. Jenny turned to look at her, but there was only darkness all around her—and silence. She began to feel afraid even though she knew

Simon and Andromeda were there. She could be completely alone. Or perhaps something else was lying in wait for her in the darkness. The house, just the other side of the panel, seemed a million light years away. It was so dark and so quiet.

But then there came something more terrifying than the silence. Suddenly in the house beyond, they heard the sound of a loud banging and the shouting of harsh voices. It was the Grey Gunners at the door, demanding entry into their house.

# 2

Simon let out a gasp when he heard the soldiers, that seemed as loud as if he had banged on the panel. He bit his lip, annoyed with himself. Andromeda put one hand on his shoulder and, with her other, gave Jenny's arm a reassuring squeeze. And despite the danger, they all felt a warm sense of peace.

They heard Mrs Miller's voice, far away but very calm, and the gruff voice of one of the Grey Gunners saying something. Then they heard the sound of feet marching through the house and many noises, which they guessed were made by the Grey Gunners searching, opening doors and drawers roughly, tearing the soft material of the chairs, banging and rapping sharply on the walls and floors.

The children waited, holding their breath. The footsteps came nearer and they could hear the hard rapping on the walls coming nearer too, until it was right over the fireplace itself. But the fireplace had been specially made so that there would be no hollow sound to give the hiding-place away. Even so, when the banging stopped abruptly, Simon felt sure a Grey Gunner would wrench the panel aside and find them.

'Nothing upstairs!' He realised another Grey Gunner had entered the room.

'I don't think there's anything in here either,' said the voice just the other side of the wall.

A third voice added, 'David Miller's one of their top men at the main military defence place. He wouldn't be stupid enough to keep any vital stuff in his house, however well hidden. There aren't any hiding-places here.'

'Finished yet?' came the gruff voice of the Commanding Officer. 'Don't waste time talking. Concentrate on the job!'

'Yes, sir. One thing, sir. What about this table? It looks as if four people have been eating here recently.'

'You're right,' replied the Commanding Officer sharply. 'Well, Mrs Miller?'

Jenny's heart began to beat faster, but she heard her mother's voice replying calmly, 'My husband had breakfast before leaving for work, well over an hour ago. As for the children, a friend came and they're with her.'

'Good for you, Mum,' thought Simon, proudly. There was a brief silence and Simon and Jenny wondered if their mother's reply would satisfy the Grey Gunners. It must have, for they heard the Commanding Officer say gruffly, 'Carry on' and then heard his voice more faintly from another part of the house, talking to somebody else.

There was the muffled sound of retreating footsteps and then the sound of voices in the hall: the officer's voice sharp and irritated; their mother's, a little annoyed but still calm. The front door banged shut and then there was silence.

For a while the children sat very still in the darkness, listening. Then Simon spoke very quietly. 'There's a light switch just inside the entrance. Shall I try and find it?' He paused. 'They may have left a couple of Gunners on guard. What do you think?'

'No. I don't think so,' said Andromeda. 'Not this time anyway. They're looking for documents, not people. But we'll wait and listen a while. See if you *can* find the light, Simon.'

After a moment or two, Simon found the light switch and, when their eyes grew accustomed to the brightness, they noticed that in the corner there was a supply of food, torches, candles and matches, as well as a few things that could be useful if they did have to stay hidden. When, after they had waited what seemed a very long time, there were no sounds at all from the house, they decided to venture out.

The house was empty, as Andromeda had thought. But when they cautiously peered through a window at the front, they saw Grey Gunners on guard in the street outside. At the back of the house, beyond the garden, was an alleyway. There were two more Gunners patrolling the alley. Simon felt his heart sink. It seemed they were trapped.

They all sat down in the room where that morning Simon and Jenny had larked about during breakfast. This time they did not sit by the windows but in a corner which could not be glimpsed from the end of the garden.

'Well,' said Simon, trying to smile, 'we're in a bit of a fix.'

'I hope Mum's all right,' said Jenny, trying not to cry. Andromeda rummaged in the large bag she had brought with her. 'I have a present for you,' she said and handed Simon a small, flat package.

'What is it?' asked Simon, brightening up.

'Open it and see, silly,' urged Jenny. 'Thank you, Andromeda.'

'Andromeda's a bit of a mouthful,' said Simon, tearing at the paper. 'I'll call you Andy if you don't mind.'

'As long as you don't call Alabaster, Ally,' Andromeda replied, smiling. A small grunting noise came from Alabaster, curled up on Andromeda's lap, as if he agreed.

The present turned out to be one of the embarrassing sort that makes you say, 'It's very nice—but what exactly is it?'

There were two slim, red folders edged with gold, and inside each folder there was a card.

'The cards explain your mission,' said Andromeda. Simon and Jenny exchanged looks of surprise.

'Mission?'

Andromeda laughed. 'Things aren't turning out quite as you thought they would at breakfast, are they? Don't worry. The King knows all about it. He's got everything under control.'

'The King has put power over everything in the hands of the Prince,' quoted Simon, remembering the strange thing Michael had said.

'You've got a good memory, Simon,' smiled Andromeda. 'The Prince is in fact your mission. I'll explain. You understand, don't you, who the Grey Gunners are?'

'They're from Gehalla. We learnt a bit about them in Cosmic History. No one knows for certain, but they're supposed to have invaded lots of planets in the next system.'

'More than that. You know this planet is one of those in the control of the Old Ruler? Well, the Grey Gunners are reinforcements for the Old Ruler's army. At one time they were part of his forces. When he conquered Gehalla, he destroyed the inhabitants and colonised it with his own people. Here he can't do that because the High King who is more powerful than he is, has forbidden him to go beyond a certain point. The Old Ruler cannot have complete control of Earth unless he deals with the King's son, the Prince.'

'The Prince!' exclaimed Jenny. 'I've heard of him, but I've never been sure if he really existed.'

'Yes. That's the main way the Old Ruler works. If people could see the Prince, share his power, then the Old Ruler would be lost. He knows that. You see, Jenny, the Prince cares for the people, but the Old Ruler loves only himself. He will stop at nothing to destroy anything and anyone who stands in his way.'

'I've never liked the sound of him,' said Simon, 'but I didn't know why.'

'That's why the King has chosen you and Jenny for this mission, Simon, because your hearts are right.'

'What exactly is this mission?' asked Simon hesitantly.

'Well, to understand it, you must know that the Grey Gunners are here to capture and kill the Prince and to discourage his followers, so that there will be no resistance to the Old Ruler taking complete control of Earth.'

Jenny shivered at the thought and Alabaster let out a plaintive miaow.

'But,' interrupted Simon, 'the Grey Gunners can't get very far, can they? They'll be picked up on the zone defence detectors and then caught or . . .'

'Simon,' countered Andromeda, 'why do you think they've landed in the conservation zone? They won't show themselves except when they have to, like today. There are so many relatively deserted areas where they can hide here. They won't be picked up on any detectors either because the only advanced technology allowed inside the zone is the video phones.'

'Yes. I see that,' protested Simon, 'but surely they'll be seen. Today, for instance, they've come in broad daylight to a street where there are people around . . .'

'Perhaps. But Simon,' broke in Andromeda, 'you don't know the Grey Gunners. Think how many rumours you've heard about them and how little fact. Believe me when I tell you they are cunning and very dangerous. You must remember that if you are to succeed in your mission. It is important that the followers of the Prince know that he is alive and that his power is greater than that of the Old Ruler. Your mission is to find the Prince before the Grey Gunners do. Do you understand?'

Simon spoke for both of them. 'Not really, but I think we can see how important it is. Only I really don't . . .'

Andromeda interrupted, smiling. 'You don't have to understand everything at once. But you've made a good start.' She took the folders from Simon. 'On this card are six messages in code, each of which will give you a clue how to find the Prince. When you find the first place you will be able to decode the second message. On this card,' she went on, pulling the second card out of its folder, 'is the code. Simon, you must keep one folder and Jenny, you must keep the other.'

'Look, Andy, I really don't think we're the best people to do this. Is it some kind of joke?'

'It must be a mistake,' joined in Jenny. 'I'd be hopeless at anything like that.'

For once Andromeda's smiling face was serious. 'The King doesn't make mistakes. He doesn't expect us to be able to do things by ourselves. He just wants us to do what he tells us and he'll take care of the rest. Anyway, although I can't do it for you, I'll be with you as long as you need me. But there's no time to waste, so let's go.'

'But we haven't had anything to eat since breakfast, except for those biscuits and the bars of chocolate in the shelter,' protested Simon.

Andromeda glanced outside at the fading light. 'All right,' she said, 'but we must be quick.' When they had raided the kitchen for some milk, bread and butter and fruit, they felt more ready to leave.

It was only then that it occurred to Simon that there was an obvious problem. 'How exactly do we get out?' he asked.

'Across the alley and into the garden the other side,' said Andromeda simply. 'Don't bring anything with you,' she said as Simon reached for a bag of odds and ends, which he felt might come in handy, 'just the folders and yourselves.'

It would have been quite simple, if Jenny had only done as she was told. As it was, all of them were placed in great danger.

By then it was twilight. They waited at the bottom of the garden until the guards were nearly at the far end of the alley. Then Simon slipped through the gate, across the alley and through the gate at the other side. Jenny followed, but she had brought with her a small pack containing a torch and some supplies, hastily gathered from the hiding-place and as she nervously crossed the alley, she dropped one of the tins.

'What was that?' One of the Gunners turned his head. Jenny had managed to dodge through the gateway and down behind the high hedge, but the treacherous tin lay in the alley.

If Andromeda had been with them, they could have asked her what to do, but she was stranded across the alleyway in their own garden. Jenny wanted to dart out and grab the tin but Simon held her back.

The Grey Gunner was walking briskly up the alley towards them. Soon he would see the tin. Crouched down behind the hedge they dared not move. They would certainly be discovered. Tears were pricking Jenny's eyes. Simon whispered, 'Nothing we can do. Perhaps the King will do something.'

'How can he?' Jenny whispered back with a sob. 'I've ruined everything. I didn't do what Andromeda said. Now we'll be caught and it will be my fault.'

Through the hedge they could see the tin almost within reach. They could not see, but they could hear the heavy footsteps of the Gunner coming nearer and nearer.

# 3

Jenny had her eyes closed tight, afraid of what might happen next, when she heard a loud and raucous miaow. She opened them to see a white cat, bright in the fading light, go tearing down the alleyway past the first Grey Gunner till, stopping by the second, he rubbed himself against his legs.

'It's only a cat,' laughed the Gunner at the far end of the alley. 'You must be getting nervous.' The other Gunner shrugged and turned away to join his comrade. He hesitated as he reached him and his eyes searched either side of the alley.

'I'm not sure that it was only a cat.' The cat purred loudly.

'Friendly old puss, aren't you?' said the other Gunner. 'Come on, we can't afford to imagine things every time we hear a noise.' So they turned away and Andromeda crossed the alley, silently picking up the tin as she went.

Jenny was trembling and almost in tears. 'I'm so sorry,' she whispered. Andromeda put her arm round her shoulders and smiled at her. 'It's all right now,' she said. 'The King rescued us that time. But it's very important that we do exactly what we are told.'

'The King?' questioned Simon. 'How?' Then before Andromeda could answer he gasped, 'The cat! It was Alabaster!'

Jenny started to say, 'Don't be silly. It was the wrong colour,' when she saw that Andromeda was nodding and that she looked pleased that Simon had guessed right. 'Don't ask me how. The King uses people, and sometimes even animals, in unexpected ways. But remember I did tell you that Alabaster was a special cat.'

A low purr from their feet told them that Alabaster had joined them again. In the last of the daylight they could see quite plainly that Alabaster was, once more, a fluffy, ordinary, black and brown cat.

'What now?' asked Simon. It was assumed that Andromeda was in charge although they had only met her that morning. She always seemed to know exactly what to do.

'We get well away from here, find a quiet place, open a couple of Jenny's tins—since she's brought them—and try to work out the first clue.'

After they had had something to eat, and had drunk water from a small, fresh stream, they all felt better and Simon and Jenny began to feel that they were actually part of an adventure. Working out the code added to the sense of excitement. It read like this:

*On the horizon, look and see*
*A fortress it was once to be.*
*Approach its danger quietly*
*Beginning at the cleft oak tree.*

'A fortress,' mused Simon. 'I can't think where that could be.'

'It could mean a castle. But there isn't one near here and if we travel to find it we don't even know which direction to go in,' added Jenny.

'I'm afraid you're on your own here,' said Andromeda. 'Read it again carefully and *think*.'

'It must be a castle or something we can see in the distance if we look round,' said Simon.

'We can't do that,' said Jenny flatly.

'Why not?' asked Simon.

'Because it's dark,' giggled Jenny.

'Silly,' said Simon. 'Anyway I don't suppose whoever

wrote the clue meant this field as the starting point.' Simon flashed the torch round about him. 'Anyway, it's flat here and there are trees all around.'

'I've got it,' said Jenny excitedly. 'To see the horizon well, you'd have to be high up.'

'Like on a hill,' added Simon, catching her excitement.

'"Approach its danger quietly

Beginning at the cleft oak tree,"' quoted Jenny. '*Beginning.*'

'At a cleft . . . maybe a tree that's been forked by lightning,' Simon joined in. He paused and he and Jenny looked at each other triumphantly. 'Of course,' said Simon, 'Holkham Hill!'

Jenny nodded. 'We have to start at the old cleft oak on Holkham Hill.'

'Well done,' said Andromeda warmly. 'Is it far?'

Simon's face fell. 'A fair way. Yes.'

'We'll think about that in the morning. But now we'd better get some sleep.'

Jenny wondered how Andromeda could possibly expect her to get to sleep out in the open, with only a log for a pillow, but she fell fast asleep almost straight away. When she woke it was still dark and she thought at first she had only slept a few minutes but, looking at the luminous face of her watch, she could see it was a little after four o'clock. She should have been frightened, but she wasn't. She knew exactly why she was awake. She flicked on the torch and shook Andromeda and Simon. Alabaster made a small growl of complaint in his sleep, but Andromeda and Simon were immediately wide awake. 'What is it?' asked Andromeda.

'I've got an idea,' said Jenny, whispering because of the darkness. Simon groaned. 'I've woken you up because I'd have to do it now, while it's still dark.'

'Whatever is it?' asked Simon, still slightly annoyed.

'Our bikes. In the garage back at the house. If we went

back and got them now, we'd stand a good chance of not being seen.'

Simon groaned again. 'Mine's not there, Jeff borrowed it for his camping holiday. One old-fashioned bike wouldn't be much good between three of us. Now if it was a question of getting our speeder bikes from home, that would be different! It's too dangerous to go back anyway.'

'One bike might do,' announced Andromeda surprisingly. 'Jenny, I think this is an idea the King has given you. You're willing to go back alone?' Without hesitating Jenny nodded. 'Then I think you should go.'

'But . . .' began Simon and the girls knew he was remembering the tin in the alleyway and how scared Jenny had been.

'Simon,' said Andromeda, silencing him, 'you've a lot to learn about the King.' She turned to Jenny. 'We'll wait for you in that little copse of trees over there.'

The dawn was just breaking, bathing the field and the woods in a pale golden mist, when Jenny returned. Her cheeks were flushed and her eyes glowed with the excitement of a mission accomplished. She had been able to ride part of the way back on her bike; now she wheeled it across the fields.

'I brought the rest of the bread and milk from the kitchen,' she said breathlessly as she reached Simon and Andromeda. So they shared an unexpected breakfast and then they started on their way.

Once they had left the village they were able to take turns at riding the bike, but Simon was still sulking over the arrangement. Andromeda was obviously disappointed at the way he was behaving, but she only said to him, 'Simon, if only you could trust him and wait and see.'

'The King?' Simon grimaced. Andromeda sighed.

Jenny, who was riding the bike, dismounted. 'You can have the rest of my turn, Simon,' she said.

'I don't want it,' said Simon rudely. 'I can't take a girl's turn anyway,' and he strode on ahead.

They were still following the road and had a little way to go before they could branch off across country. Simon was some way ahead; Jenny was undecided whether she should remount the bike (and taking turns hadn't really been successful as the rider had a long wait for the other two to catch up) and Andromeda was standing motionless, her head bent and her hands clasped together.

So they weren't even together to decide what to do, when the crisis came. Suddenly, without warning, a car came racing along the road from the direction in which they had come. The land at the roadside was flat and provided no hiding-place. In any case it was too late. They had been seen.

Jenny half wondered if she should pedal furiously across country to reach Holkham Hill alone, but the car was already drawing level with them and stopping. Ahead of them Simon turned back, ashamed that he wasn't with the girls to protect them if this turned out to be the Grey Gunners. Jenny looked at Alabaster, a warm bundle of black and brown fur, curled up in the basket on her bike. It didn't look as if there was to be any help from him this time.

But strangely enough help came from the car. It obviously wasn't the Grey Gunners after all, but there was a cautious exchange between the family in the car and the children before they discovered they were all in the same boat.

The man was one of their father's colleagues and they were trying to get to the isolated house of a relative before the Grey Gunners tracked them down.

'Where are you going?' the father asked.

Jenny hesitated. 'Across country,' replied Andromeda.

'On foot!' he exclaimed anxiously. 'Listen, your dad would never forgive me if I left you like this. I know we can't give you a lift, but I have the kids' bikes strapped on the roof. We won't need them when we get to the border. You take them.'

The two children in the back nodded enthusiastically. 'It's great to be able to help each other at a time like this,' said the boy as he helped his father unstrap the bikes.

When they had gone, the children stared at each other. Andromeda smiled. Simon was the first to speak. 'I feel dreadful. I really do. All that fuss I made and now this.'

'It's the King again, isn't it?' said Jenny in a hushed voice.

'That's what makes it so awful,' exclaimed Simon. 'I have the feeling that he had this in mind all along, even while I was moaning away.'

'Well, Simon,' said Andromeda, 'try saying sorry, then saying thank you and then making a new start!'

Despite himself Simon began to smile and soon all three of them were racing along as if they were blown by the wind. After stopping for lunch with the last of the tins, and a tea of wild berries, at dusk they reached Holkham Hill. They dismounted and wheeled their bikes up to the large, dark shape of the cleft oak.

'Pity we'll have to wait till morning to see anything, let alone the horizon,' said Simon, trying to get his breath back.

'Hush,' said Jenny urgently. Andromeda stood pale and still, clutching the handlebars of her bike.

'What's the matter?' asked Simon in a low voice. Then he looked where the girls were looking and saw the pin-pricks of light a short distance away all around them in the growing darkness. He had never seen anything like it before, but he knew instantly what it was. They had unknowingly walked straight into a trap. For those lights belonged to Gehallen shelters. Inside the shelters were the Grey Gunners. They had walked right into the enemy camp.

# 4

It was very still in the camp and very quiet. Simon was puzzled. How had they managed to get right into the middle of the camp without getting caught? Where was the enemy now? It was too early for them to be sleeping but it was very strange how there was no sound or movement at all from the shelters.

Then Simon, who had only just promised Andromeda that he would make a new start, made the most terrible mistake of the whole adventure. He thought because it was all quiet that the camp must be deserted. He forgot all about thinking what the King might want them to do, or asking Andromeda's advice or anything like that and began creeping down the hill towards the nearest shelter.

If he had seen Alabaster jump down from the bicycle basket, arch his back and hiss at the darkness, he might have thought twice about there being any danger.

Andromeda bent to stroke Alabaster and as she did so she put her hand on Jenny's arm and shook her head. Jenny understood that Andromeda meant she must not try and stop Simon. Then Andromeda put her finger to her lips to signal that they dare not even whisper.

Jenny crouched down beside her in the shadow of the huge tree and for a little while they held their breath and waited.

There was enough light left just to make out the shapes of the shelters and of some clumps of trees and bushes. Andromeda touched Jenny's arm and pointed to a clump of overhanging bushes, thick with creeper which sprawled across a small hollow in the ground. Then she pointed to the bikes. Jenny nodded. She was beginning to see how the King was meeting their needs in the strangest ways. The bushes provided a perfect hiding place for the three bikes, and, because of the hollow, the girls were able to get them hidden without a great deal of rustling of leaves and branches.

Jenny almost began to feel that Simon would be so well protected that a Grey Gunner wouldn't see him either. But she was wrong there.

With the bikes safely hidden, Jenny and Andromeda were able to crouch down inside the hollow where the great oak tree had split. They had only just settled in when a strange and frightening thing happened to the whole hilltop. Suddenly there was a loud wailing noise and immediately the entire hillside was ablaze with lights and there was the sound of running footsteps and voices shouting.

They knew immediately what had happened. Simon must have triggered off an alarm, and wherever the Grey Gunners had been before, now they were all here! They heard Simon's voice yelling, 'Let me go. Let me go.'

Then there was some scuffling and a voice saying, 'It's only a boy.'

Then another voice they recognised as the gruff voice of the Commanding Officer who had taken their mother away said, 'No, not *a* boy—*the* boy. It's Miller's son. Take him to the Treatment Room.'

Simon seemed to have lost his voice. Jenny risked peeping out and saw the group in the artificial light, a little distance away. Simon was being marched away by two Grey Gunners.

Then Jenny had the worst moment she had had yet—worse even than when she had dropped the tin. For, seeing Simon being led away and not being able to talk to Andromeda, Jenny began to wonder about the whole mission. She began to wonder why the King had let them walk into this trap; wondered if it was worth trying to reach the Prince and, worst of all, she began to feel that nothing was worthwhile any more and they might as well give themselves up to the Grey Gunners and have done with it.

Then Andromeda whispered the only thing to which Jenny would have paid any attention, 'Alabaster's gone.'

'What!' mouthed Jenny, looking round. Andromeda got up. 'Come on, Jenny. I think this side of the camp is safe. They all went that way. Let's look for him.'

Searching for an animal in that strange, dark place, was quite hopeless. There was no sign of Alabaster. But they did find some food, enough to eat and to store for the next day's journey.

'What do we do now, Andy?' whispered Jenny. 'Do we try and get away or rescue Simon?'

Andromeda was silent for a long while, her head bent. Jenny was about to ask a second time when Andromeda spoke. 'At the bottom of the hill there is a ruined house by a small stream. We will try and get the bikes there and wait for Simon.'

'You think Simon will come?' Jenny forgot how awful she had felt only a few moments ago and she began to feel the stirring of new hope and the old excitement.

'We'll both take a bike,' went on Andromeda, 'and then I'll come back for . . .' She stopped speaking and flattened herself against the wall of the nearest shelter. 'They're coming back,' she whispered so quietly that Jenny barely caught what she said. Then she heard the voices and the footsteps. Two dark shapes crossed the hilltop towards the shelter, where they stood in shadow—Grey Gunners.

It was the first time Jenny had seen them as close as this. She had not realised how tall they were and how strong they must be. Their grey skin made them look like men of iron in the artificial light. 'What if they discover the food is gone?' she thought suddenly. 'What if they see us?'

Then that same feeling of peace she had felt the first day in the hiding place came.

A voice called, 'Alker, Draken!' The Gunners stopped. 'What's he want now?' one of them grumbled.

'Let's go on. They can call again if they want,' said the other.

'And risk the Treatment Room! Not likely,' said the first, turning.

The other hesitated, then he too turned, mumbling, 'Better go and see what's up now.'

Andromeda and Jenny knew that they would have to move quickly; they had so nearly been caught. So, very carefully and quietly, they got two of the bikes and steered them in between the shelters down the hillside.

With great relief they arrived at the ruined house. Andromeda stopped a moment, listening, but Jenny left her bike and went inside, anxious to be out of sight. A few seconds later she screamed.

Andromeda rushed round the corner. Then she stopped abruptly and burst out laughing. Immediately hands released Jenny and she fell forward. 'Andy,' said a shocked voice. Jenny turned to see who had held her captive.

'Simon!' she gasped. 'Oh, Simon!'

When they had all recovered from the shock, Simon told his story. He had stumbled on a great underground complex with some strange machines and weapons. He had been so amazed that he hadn't heard two Gunners come up behind him. The girls told him of the part they had seen and overheard.

'After that,' said Simon, 'I thought they were going to torture me to make me talk. I never felt so frightened in my life. But they just shut me up in this little room. I think they were waiting for somebody to arrive.'

'The Old Ruler,' breathed Andromeda, her eyes wide.

'Anyway, I was sitting with my head in my hands, when I just felt there was somebody in the room with me. I was almost afraid to look up. When I did I saw there really was someone there, but it wasn't a Grey Gunner. It was a cloaked figure and he said, "Simon, don't be afraid. Follow me." He said it very quietly, but firmly, so I didn't argue. I followed him and he walked out of the room and down the hillside to the stream. Then he said to me, "You must cross the stream alone," and then he added a funny thing: "But remember I'm always with you,"—and he disappeared. Then I heard you come.'

'He is quite amazing,' exclaimed Andromeda.

'Who?' chorused Simon and Jenny. There was a catch in her voice as she turned to Simon. 'Do you know who rescued you, Simon?'

Simon shook his head. 'I hadn't met him before.'

'It was the Prince,' announced Andromeda. 'It could have been no one else.'

'The P-prince!' stammered Simon.

'The Prince?' echoed Jenny.

'He walked right into the enemy camp just to rescue you, Simon.' Simon sat down stunned. A sudden idea struck Jenny.

'Then we won't finish our mission,' she said sadly. 'The Prince knows about the invasion and the Grey Gunners being after him.'

Andromeda said surprisingly, 'He's known all along. Remember, Simon "The King has put power over everything in the hands of the Prince." He doesn't *need* to use us for his mission, but he has his own reasons for doing so. We don't need to understand, just to obey.'

There was nothing more to be said after that. They took turns to keep watch while each of them had an hour's sleep. It was strange that although the enemy would be bound to have discovered Simon's escape, not a single one of the Grey Gunners of Gehalla came out of the camp in pursuit. But it was cautiously that they set off while it was still dark, aiming to be out of sight of Holkham Hill by daylight.

The children had a pleasant and uneventful journey across the moonlit plain to the fortress which, they had discovered from decoding the second clue, lay in a direct line due west from the ruined house. The clue also told them that the fortress was called the Green Tower. But that was all.

When they first saw the tower bathed in the rosy and golden light of dawn, it looked very romantic, like something out of a fairy tale. Close up, in the cold, clear light of early morning, it looked awesome. It was built of large, thick blocks of grey stone, which were mostly covered by a green creeper.

On the ground level was a stout, wooden door and two windows. High up there was only one small window, almost covered with creeper. The tower looked very old and broken down, but they knew better by now than to assume it was empty.

'Better work out the next clue before we do anything,' said Simon, who was learning at last.

He jumped as a woman's voice, sharp and loud called, 'Simon! Come on, I know you're there. Come out and show yourself or there'll be trouble!'

Jenny happened to be looking up at the high window just then or she might have missed seeing a bird fly down. She thought she had seen a hand release the bird.

'Andy,' she said, 'there's a bird,' and she pointed to the tree where it had landed. Andromeda walked quietly to the tree and coaxed down the strange little dove, with the colours of the rainbow on his breast. Attached to his leg was a rough piece of paper and scratched on it with some thick, dark stuff, she could just make out the words: 'Please rescue me'. She looked up at the empty window.

Just then the harsh voice came again, 'Simon! Simon!' and suddenly the thick wooden door swung open.

# 5

A huge woman stood there, scowling around her. Her large hands were placed threateningly on her wide hips.

'Where's that boy?' she thundered, seeming to look directly at the clump of bushes where the children were hidden. Jenny trembled and Simon stood as if fixed to the ground, his mouth hanging open. Then, as if it were some fairy tale turning into a nightmare reality, out from the tower behind her came a man even larger than the woman, big and broad with scowling black brows.

'You haven't lost the boy?' he growled down at her.

The woman sat down on a wooden seat and (Jenny was so tense at this point that she nearly had a fit of giggles) took out some knitting. 'Oh, he's just hiding again. I'm not wasting my time looking for him. He'll turn up when he's hungry enough.'

'Nuisance of a boy,' growled the 'giant' again and stretched himself out on a second wooden seat on the opposite side of the door. 'I'll be glad when we can hand him over to the Grey Gunners.'

Simon, by now, was almost beside himself with fright. Andromeda touched his arm and whispered, 'I don't think they mean you.' She motioned to Simon and Jenny to follow her until they were well out of earshot of the tower. 'Simon,' she said sharply, 'remember you are on a mission. You will never complete it if you give in like this to the least sign of possible danger. Now come on, where are your folders? We must look at the next clue.' Simon handed her his folder in silence.

Jenny's eyes sparkled as she fished out her folder.

'Andy,' she said, unable to suppress her excitement though she felt sorry for Simon, 'is it the Prince do you think, the prisoner?'

The thought had obviously not occurred to Simon and he began to brighten up. Then he relapsed into a sulk again mumbling, 'Perhaps it's a trap.'

Andromeda laughed. 'Oh, Simon!' Then she sighed. 'I really don't think the warder and his wife are that clever. Big yes, but not clever. But I don't know what we're going to do with you.'

Simon began to relax as they looked at the clue and by the time they had solved it, the old excitement was coming back and he was beginning to feel ashamed of the way he had behaved. The clue read:

*The boy like a bird*
*Longs to be free.*
*The prison is locked,*
*But the boy holds a key.*

This time it was Jenny's turn to be disappointed. 'It doesn't sound as if it's the Prince then. Just a boy. Why doesn't he get out by himself if he's got a key?'

Andromeda was beginning to lose patience with the pair of them. 'Jenny,' she sighed again, 'remember it was you who saw the rainbow dove. You wanted to help then, no matter who it was, not just if it was the Prince. Remember this is a clue, a pointer. It doesn't give us all the facts. Remember how we worked out the clue about the tower. Well, this clue tells us one very important thing now. Perhaps it will tell us another later. Do you know what it is?'

'That the boy wants to be free,' said Jenny quietly.

'That's true,' said Andromeda, 'but more important than that, it tells us,' she paused to look at Simon, 'that this is not a trap. It tells us that the next step in our mission is to rescue the boy.'

'Yes,' agreed Simon, seeing it all fall into place. 'Hey,' he exclaimed, 'perhaps this boy's called Simon too!'

'Let's go and find out,' said Andromeda and she turned and led them back to the tower.

'But we haven't made any plans,' protested Simon as they went. Jenny shrugged, following close on Andromeda's heels.

The warder was asleep, but his wife sat busily clicking her knitting needles. Again Jenny had to fight the urge to giggle. She looked up at the window where she had seen the rainbow dove and gasped, for there was a face looking down at them. A pair of hands signalled urgently. This time Andromeda saw the prisoner too.

Simon chose that moment to step on a twig. The clicking of the knitting needles stopped abruptly and the warder's wife looked up. But instead of looking at the bushes, from where the noise had come, she turned and looked at the tower. The face at the window disappeared a fraction of a second too late.

The warder's wife was up and through the door in less time than you could have imagined so large a bulk could move. 'The boy,' she screeched, prodding her husband awake as she went. 'Simon,' she shouted, 'just you wait till I catch you.'

Our Simon caught Andromeda's eye and gave a knowing look. They did not have to wait long to see his namesake. The warder's wife reappeared, dragging him after her.

'Here he is, the good for nothing wretch. What's to be done with him now?' she gloated.

And a wretch he did look. His clothes were ragged and dirty, his eyes huge and frightened in his thin face. The warder barely disturbed himself from his comfortable position. 'The dungeon again,' he growled briefly.

By now the children should have been used to strange things happening, but each new demonstration of the King's power caught them by surprise.

Suddenly, it seemed from nowhere, a huge white panther sprang across the bushes to land in the clearing in front of the tower. Its eyes glinted dangerously and its sharp teeth and claws looked deadly.

The warder and his wife, not to mention the boy, were certainly very much afraid. The warder was up off the grass and into the tower quicker than you could say, 'Hello, white panther' and his wife behind him. They bolted the door, leaving the boy alone outside with the panther.

Jenny had felt that, from the first moment she had seen the rainbow dove at the window, somehow the responsibility for the rescue was hers. So she did a very brave thing. She rushed into the clearing, where the panther was prowling towards the boy, grabbed him and pulled him into the bushes.

When she looked back to the clearing she was amazed to see that the panther had gone. She turned to Andromeda, who smiled at her with approval. Jenny was surprised, and yet not surprised, to see Alabaster in Andromeda's arms, purring softly as she stroked him.

'The panther?' asked Jenny, 'Was it . . .?'

Andromeda nodded. 'Yes, it was Alabaster.'

'Wow!' said Simon, who could think of nothing else to say.

They had to get well away from the tower before the boy would stop trembling and sit down quietly. Sitting calmly, they wished they had something to give the boy to eat. In fact they all felt rather hungry. And suddenly Jenny felt tired too. All this excitement and no sleep and no food, not to mention a ragged boy to look after, suddenly seemed too much.

'Well,' Andromeda asked the boy, 'what has the King said to you?'

Jenny and Simon looked at each other in surprise. The boy studied each of them in turn and finally his eyes fell on

Simon's small red folder. He smiled in relief. 'Power over everything is still in the hands of the Prince,' he said slowly.

'You have been with the Prince?' asked Andromeda.

The boy smiled and looked down at his hands. 'That is not why they took me. They want me to tell them where he can be found. I will not. Even though the Grey Gunners use their methods on me, I will not tell.'

'You are safe now,' said Andromeda and she made a sign in the grass.

The boy relaxed completely and nodded. 'Yes,' he said, 'safe and free.'

'The key,' recalled Simon. 'Why didn't you use the key to get out?'

The boy looked at him blankly. 'The key?'

Then Jenny burst in excitedly, 'I've got it. It's not a key to open doors, is it? It's the kind of key to unlock mysteries, isn't it, Andromeda? It's the key to what we do next.'

'Of course,' said Simon. 'Why didn't I think of that!'

'We're on a mission for the King,' explained Andromeda to the boy, 'and it seems that only you can tell us what to do next.'

'We're trying to find the Prince,' added Jenny.

The boy nodded. 'Yes, I know where we must go.'

'We have these clues to follow,' said Simon, taking the card out of his folder.

'May I see?' asked the boy.

Simon nodded and pointed out the fourth clue. The boy looked at the clue and read out, not the jumble of letters but the meaning. Simon and Jenny looked at him open-mouthed. Andromeda smiled. 'It comes from being with the Prince. Read it again.'

So he read:

*When the traveller through time is lost to sight,*
*Power will flash through the deep coloured light.*
*When the children of light learn to travel alone,*
*He will always be with them and the Prince will be home.*

'My goodness,' exclaimed Jenny, 'whatever does that mean?'

'I don't understand it,' said Simon, 'but I think when the things happen, whatever they are, that the Prince will be safe and our mission finished.'

Jenny shrugged her shoulders but Andromeda nodded. 'In a way you're right, but in another way your mission will only be beginning then.'

The boy stood up. 'I will take you,' he said. They left the bicycles hidden in some bushes and went by foot across country. They crossed several meadows and went into a wood. Andromeda suggested they rest for a while and, if possible, have something to eat. They found blackberries and nuts and even a small stream of fresh water. In the leafy coolness of the wood, with the warm sun filtering through the branches, Jenny felt excitement stir inside her. They were on their way to see the Prince at last.

They came out on a small hilltop. The boy stopped and pointed across the plain. The peaceful patchwork of fields in the afternoon sunshine looked a fit place to end their journey.

But, as they started down the hill, a shadow came between them and the sun. A strange, high noise broke the quiet of the countryside. They had forgotten what the warder had said about the Grey Gunners coming; forgotten all about Gehalla and the forces of the Old Ruler until, right in their pathway, so that there could be no possible escape, they saw the spaceship land.

# 6

The noise of the spaceship landing was quite deafening. Simon and Jenny were almost blown off their feet by the force of air from the slip-stream. They were so busy just trying to keep on their feet that they didn't notice what was happening to Andromeda and the boy.

Andromeda, with Alabaster in her arms, was standing as still as if she had been turned to stone. But the boy was lying motionless on the ground.

As suddenly as it had begun, the noise stopped. The sun was still shining and the countryside was still beautiful, but now it all seemed different. It was the kind of strange sensation that sometimes comes when you feel very afraid of something. Everything else suddenly seems very unreal and the only real things are you and the terrible thing you are afraid of. That's exactly how it was with Jenny and Simon. They were alone in the world with the huge, metallic spaceship looming in front of them. They watched as if hypnotised, waiting for the door to open and the Grey Gunners to walk out.

Then for the third time, this time for both Jenny and Simon, the feeling of peace, which seemed to be a very special gift from the King, came over them. A few moments later the door of the spaceship swung open and suddenly everything changed.

Andromeda was the first to move. Like a princess released from a magic spell, she ran towards the spaceship. The figure who had climbed out of the spaceship took his helmet off and Simon and Jenny saw that it was not a Grey Gunner at all. It was Michael—Michael who had brought

Andromeda to them in the first place, Michael whom they had liked so much from the first moment they met him.

He held out his arms to Andromeda. 'Well done,' he said. 'Well done.'

Then he turned to Simon and Jenny and shook them each by the hand. 'I see you've both grown since I last saw you. No, not taller. A bit wiser, a bit better, more like our Prince. I can see it in your faces. But who's this?' he asked, looking beyond them to the boy lying on the ground.

Andromeda smiled reassuringly at Jenny across the still figure.

'He'll be all right. He's just very tired and weak. He probably hasn't eaten properly for days. He's a servant of the Prince,' she explained to Michael, 'another Simon.'

'Then he must come and be cared for,' said Michael and he lifted him and carried him into the spaceship.

While he was gone Andromeda clasped first Jenny's hands, then Simon's. There were tears in her eyes as she struggled to speak. Finally she said, 'You're doing well, very well, both of you. Remember everything we've learnt together won't you and don't forget . . .'

That was all she said then, for Michael joined them. He put his arm round Andromeda's shoulders, but it was to Simon and Jenny that he spoke. 'You're nearly at journey's end now. But it's a journey you must finish alone. This is the only help we can give you towards the next stage of the journey,' he went on, handing to each of them a small parcel, which they guessed contained food supplies. 'But you will find that it is enough. We'll meet again soon. Goodbye, Jenny. Goodbye, Simon.' Once more he shook each of them by the hand, then turned towards the spaceship with Andromeda.

When they reached it, Michael turned and called, 'Don't forget! The King has put power over everything in the hands of the Prince!' Then he helped Andromeda into the spaceship and climbed in himself. The door swung to, hiding them from sight. There was the same loud, roaring noise again as the spaceship rose into the air. And then suddenly they were gone.

Simon and Jenny were still standing where they had been when the spaceship first came into sight. Now the countryside was bright with the warm sunshine again and the danger they had feared was gone, but they both felt so sad that they did not want to move or speak.

Finally Jenny said, 'Alabaster?' and hope crept back into her voice. 'I didn't see Alabaster go.'

Simon hesitated, then he said as gently as he could, 'I'm afraid he did, Jenny. He jumped into the spaceship when Michael carried Simon in.'

'Oh,' said Jenny in a small voice. She sank slowly to the ground and buried her head in her hands and cried. Simon sat down quietly beside her. It's not so easy for boys to cry. He swallowed the lump in his throat and stared hard into the distance.

'Come on, we've still got a mission to finish,' said Simon at last, remembering what Andromeda had said to him at the Green Tower. 'My goodness, what would Andromeda say if she could see us sitting here?'

For the first time Jenny smiled. 'She'd tell us to get on with it.'

'Right,' said Simon, feeling more confident. 'Off we go.'

'Where?' asked Jenny pointedly.

For a moment Simon was taken aback, then he said, 'We'll carry on downhill, look for somewhere to shelter for the night and eat our food. We know we're in the right place because the other Simon brought us here—and there's nothing we can do about the last clue until it happens to us.'

'Simon,' said Jenny, jumping to her feet and grabbing his arm. 'The clue! It *is* happening.'

'What!' cried Simon, taken aback.

'Yes. Remember the first line. "When the traveller through time is lost to sight." It's Andy. Don't you think so, Simon? The traveller through time is Andy.'

'Yes,' said Simon slowly. 'Yes, I think you're right. And now she's lost to sight. What's the next line?'

'"Power will flash through the deep coloured light."'

The children looked eagerly around them. Everything was pale and still in the cool light of early evening, but the excitement was with them as they hurried down the hillside.

As they neared the valley, they saw a house not too far away. They hurried towards it with thoughts of a hot drink, fresh food and even warm beds. They began to feel that the King was looking after them after all. Jenny almost cried with disappointment when they got to the house and found that it, like the house by the stream, was a ruin.

'Probably the Grey Gunners,' said Simon. Jenny looked at him, her eyes wide. 'Well, at least they're not here now,' he added quickly.

'I'm cold and I'm hungry,' said Jenny.

'We've got the parcels Michael gave us and we've still got the torch,' said Simon trying to stay cheerful. He perhaps shouldn't have said it for, just as the darkness was beginning to close in, the light of the torch began to flicker and suddenly they were plunged into total darkness. Simon could no longer think of anything cheerful to say. He dreaded having to cope with Jenny if she started crying again. He was relieved to hear her speak quite calmly.

'Simon, I've just remembered what Michael said. You know, about how we'd grown. I think he's right. I think the King lets these things happen to us because it gives us a chance to act properly, to learn to be better.'

Simon, forgetting Jenny couldn't see him, nodded in agreement.

Suddenly the sky was split by a flash of light, which was

like nothing Simon and Jenny had ever seen. It seemed to have in it all the colours of the rainbow. For a few seconds it lit up the whole countryside in the colours it would have had on the warmest, clearest, sunny day.

'It's beautiful,' gasped Jenny.

'The deep coloured light!' exclaimed Simon.

Then it was dark again, but the children felt different. They felt warm inside, happy and eager to set off to find the Prince. Neither of them wanted to talk about how they felt, but each of them sensed that the other felt exactly the same.

'Shall we open Michael's parcels?' suggested Simon.

It was a fine game tearing off the paper in the dark and trying to guess by poking and sniffing what food they had to eat. There were sandwiches, cake and fruit as well as a small flask of fruit juice each to drink. It tasted wonderful, like nothing they had ever tasted before. They weren't sure if this was because Michael had given them food from his native planet, or whether it was because they were concentrating on the taste, not being able to see anything, or perhaps it was simply because they felt so happy. It could even have been a combination of all three.

'In the morning then, we'll go on,' said Simon, when they had finished.

'Yes,' replied Jenny and within minutes they were both sound asleep.

When they set off in the brisk morning air, they seemed to know, without talking about it, which direction to take.

'Hey, Simon,' said Jenny, 'we can look at the rest of the clue now, can't we?'

'So we can,' said Simon, pulling his folder out of his pocket. 'Well, I'm blowed,' he said as he found it. 'Listen, Jenny.

"When the children of light learn to travel alone,"'

'That's what we're doing,' interrupted Jenny, 'travelling alone. So the children of light must be us. Go on.'

'"He will always be with them and the Prince will be home."'

'Oh. I don't understand the last bit,' said Jenny, disappointed.

'Well I do,' said Simon. 'It's exactly what the Prince said to me when I crossed the stream.'

'After he'd rescued you from the Grey Gunners?'

'Yes. He said I'd have to cross the stream alone, but he added the funny bit I didn't understand then, that he'd always be with me. The way he's with me isn't like you're with me. It's something to do with the way we both feel inside, the way we feel we can tackle anything right now.'

'Even Grey Gunners,' said Jenny smiling.

'We couldn't do it if we didn't feel he was with us,' said Simon solemnly.

'We have rather messed things up once or twice,' said Jenny ruefully. 'And the Prince is home?' she added.

'Yes, safe with the King.'

'I don't understand. Our mission is finished then?'

'Don't you see, Jenny, what our mission is?'

'No,' replied Jenny, puzzled. 'I don't.'

'It's to take the news back where the Grey Gunners are. It's to tell the people that the Prince is safe. In a way we have found the Prince. Now we must tell people what he's done for us and share his power with them. That's the only thing that'll make the Old Ruler fall flat on his face and send the Grey Gunners packing, back to Gehalla.'

'Yes,' said Jenny, slowly. 'I see.'

Then they smelt, quite unmistakably, eggs and bacon. Nothing smells quite as good as eggs and bacon in the early morning. It smells especially good if you haven't eaten a hot meal for days.

Jenny and Simon followed their noses which led them to an old farmhouse, with a flower garden ablaze with colour. They were very hungry, but careful enough not to rush in. They hid behind the garage and from there they could almost see through the large kitchen window.

They both had to bite their lips to stop themselves from yelling out, for, sitting at the table, eating breakfast, were their father and mother.

Simon and Jenny were learning well, and the power of the Prince was protecting them well for, just as they were about to leave the shelter of the garage, a Grey Gunner walked across the yard. They could see now that there was a Grey Gunner in the kitchen too. Jenny and Simon were even able to smile this time, a we-might-have-known kind of smile. At least they knew their parents were safe, even though they had walked bang into the Grey Gunners again.

Jenny quavered for a moment. 'If only Andromeda . . .' she began.

Simon shook his head. 'Silly. The *Prince* is with us. He'll go on guiding us, step by step. We're by ourselves now, but soon there'll be others who'll join us.'

'Mum and Dad?' asked Jenny, gaining confidence.

Simon nodded. 'Looks like the next part of the mission is to rescue them. Yes,' Simon went on as a plan suddenly came to him. 'Listen, Jenny, this is what we'll do.'

# 7

Jenny was tempted to say, 'Remember the last time we walked into a camp full of Grey Gunners!' Just thinking about Simon being dragged off to the Treatment Room brought back the fear and doubt she had felt in the grim darkness on Holkham Hill.

She glanced uneasily round her, half expecting a Grey Gunner to march round the corner of the garage. The confidence she had felt a moment ago was suddenly gone. She felt the tears welling up in her eyes as she turned to Simon. 'Not here,' she said, her mouth trembling, 'Wait until we're somewhere safe.' Simon was afraid that she was going to burst into tears at any minute, so he acted quickly with a lot more confidence that he would have had if he had stopped to think about the pickle they were in.

Taking a careful look round the corner of the garage and a quick glance through the kitchen window, he looked round for the best place to go. To the left of the shed and away from the farmhouse was a small orchard, bounded by a stone wall. In the wall was a wooden gate and beyond it the land dipped down before it opened out in a patchwork of fields, golden, brown and green as far as the eye could see.

'Through the gate,' thought Simon as he took Jenny firmly by the hand and they both half ran, half crept to the shelter of a large chestnut tree. From there they reached the orchard and edged their way, under cover of the trees, until they were almost at the wall. Then Simon darted quickly to the gate, while Jenny kept watch. He unlatched the gate and moved swiftly through the gateway. Jenny left the tree and ran till she reached Simon. Then she collapsed, trembling next to him behind the wall.

Simon closed his eyes and sighed deeply. 'We did it, Jenny. Nobody spotted us.' Jenny felt a small, warm feeling of relief inside, though her legs suddenly felt like jelly.

'Yes,' she said and tried to smile, while two large tears rolled down her cheeks.

But they were wrong. They had been spotted. Their escape across the yard to the chestnut tree, across the orchard and through the gateway had not been completely unobserved.

At the exact moment that Simon had glanced through the window, the Grey Gunner had turned away to pour out some coffee. Mrs Miller was staring at the half-eaten bowl of cornflakes in front of her, suddenly remembering that breakfast with Simon and Jenny, the morning it had all begun.

Mr Miller was putting a forkful of bacon and egg in his mouth when he suddenly felt as if someone was watching him through the window. For days the Grey Gunners had watched him and Mrs Miller almost without a break, yet he felt that this was something different. All this happened very quickly. Not quickly enough for him to catch Simon's eye, but just in time for him to glimpse two brown heads, and a flash of blue shirt and red dress, before the heads ducked down out of sight and disappeared, leaving only the usual view of the red brick garage.

Mr Miller glanced across at his wife. She sat motionless, still staring at her cereal bowl and he could see that she looked as if she was about to cry. He wished he could stretch out his hand and squeeze hers reassuringly. He longed too to lean over and look out of the window to see if there was any sign of what he thought he had seen. But he did neither.

The Grey Gunner was returning to the table with three

cups of coffee. Mr Miller cut another portion of egg and pushed it on to the bacon on his fork, as if he had nothing on his mind but his breakfast. There was no outward sign that his heart was pounding and his mind was racing. He felt the first surge of excitement and hope since he had been taken prisoner. That one brief glimpse had been enough. He was certain it was Simon and Jenny.

Mrs Miller blinked away her tears and looked up at her husband. She was surprised to see a glimmer of excitement in his brown eyes, as if he was trying to signal some good news to her. But she thought she could only have imagined it, for he simply turned to the Grey Gunner and said 'Thank you,' evenly, as he took the coffee.

Simon leaned back against the smooth, warm stones of the wall and looked at the horizon far in the distance. He deliberately avoided looking at Jenny, though he felt her misery and fear, like the claws of a frightened cat, digging into him. It seemed to him at that moment, that the whole responsibility of the mission was on his shoulders. Even knowing that his parents were near didn't help, because seeing them guarded and helpless made him feel that there was no one in the world he could turn to now. He didn't feel like sharing his plan to rescue them, just to have it quashed by Jenny. In fact, he had had enough of the whole adventure.

Perhaps Simon and Jenny shouldn't have been feeling like this, when they had had so many signs to show them that the King was looking after them and had even now led them to the place where their parents were imprisoned. They could have been remembering the rainbow dove, Michael's encouraging words from the spaceship, or the bright coloured light of the night before. They could have been feeling excited at the thought of rescuing their parents.

But they were tired and hungry and they were still very new at learning to do what the King wanted them to do.

More than that, they were fighting forces they knew nothing about as they trespassed on territory held by the Grey Gunners of Gehalla. They needed the King to do something special before they would be ready to go on to the next stage of their mission.

But what the King did was probably not at all the kind of thing they would have chosen. In fact it was probably the last thing they felt they could have faced at that moment.

As they sat in the early morning sunshine, leaning against the wall, each wrapped in their own problems and misery, they heard—faintly at first and then louder—the sound of voices. Jenny felt a sinking feeling in the pit of her stomach. Not Grey Gunners. Not now. But not only were there Grey Gunners in the orchard, they were making their way to the wall.

Simon wished he had had the sense to have moved further away from the gate before he and Jenny had sat down. The voices were very near now. Pressing the side of his face against the wall, Simon looked up to see an elbow in grey uniform, leaning against the wall. For a moment he felt everything spin around him. He took a deep breath, then another and concentrated on keeping as still as he could.

But something very different was happening to Jenny. It was as if something inside her snapped. 'Why go on fighting them?' she thought. Why not just give herself up to the Grey Gunners? There would be food. She would be with her mother and father again. The running and the hiding would be over. After all, they hadn't actually seen the Grey Gunners do anything bad. Yes, that would be the best thing to do, to give herself up to the Grey Gunners. Jenny pressed her hands down on the ground and slowly began to ease herself up on to her feet.

# 8

It was a good thing Simon didn't call out or try and grab Jenny when she stood up, because the Grey Gunner leaning against the wall would certainly have spun round at the slightest sound—and then they would both have been caught. Jenny's movements in the soft grass made no noise at all. She had really expected the Grey Gunners to see her the moment she stood up, so she was a little taken aback when they merely carried on talking. She wondered if she should make a noise, or walk through the gate so they couldn't fail to see her.

There was still part of her mind free from the awful spell that had caught hold of her so that, as she made her choice, she thought of Simon. If she made a noise and the Gunners turned, then they would see Simon too. That wouldn't be fair to Simon. Up till now she had been so bound up in her own miserable thoughts that she had only thought of the Grey Gunners' talking as a chance to give herself up. Now, for the first time, she actually heard the words they were saying.

'If the kids haven't turned up by tomorrow, I think he should be taken to the Treatment Room.' This was the Gunner leaning on the wall, his back to Jenny.

There was only one other Gunner with him and he was sitting on the grass. He was peeling the bark of a stick with a small knife, not trying to create anything, but as if he enjoyed hurting and spoiling things. Jenny could not see him, but she heard the bitterness in his voice as he spoke.

'He hasn't got anything to tell us. Why should we feed

them and humour them? The Treatment Room would be entertaining, but it would be a waste of time. We should get rid of them—both of them.'

He flicked the knife shut and sprang to his feet. 'As for the kids,' he said, 'I wouldn't have thought they're worth the trouble Malek is going to. If we came across them, of course,' he added grimly as he turned towards his companion, 'it would be as well to be rid of them too.'

Jenny dropped out of sight. It was not because she was being particularly quick-witted or clever, but because the shock of what she had heard was so great that her legs almost gave way under her. She and Simon looked at each other, hardly daring to breathe, as they heard what their fate would be if they were caught now.

'Well, it's not up to us,' said the first Gunner, straightening up to move away from the wall. 'This isn't one of the extermination missions you're used to in the ZX Division. This is something altogether different. It needs brains as well as brawn. You could mess everything up by not following orders.' His voice already sounded a little distance away. 'Take some advice from someone who's had experience in these inter-planetary affairs and don't try and outwit the Generals—or you'll end up in the Treatment Room.'

After that there was silence. The Gunner who had been speaking had obviously gone, though they could pick up no sound of retreating footsteps. From the other Gunner there was no sound to indicate what he was doing. They waited for some kind of reaction to the crushing parting remarks of the other Gunner, but there was only this strange silence. Of course, he might have quietly walked away, but they felt that this was very unlikely. Simon felt a prickle of fear, which made it almost impossible to keep still. He began to feel absolutely convinced that, if he tilted his head back, and looked up, he would find the Grey Gunner looking down at them. In his mind's eye he could see clearly the grey face, leering at them, like a hunter gloating over two animals caught in a trap.

Nothing at all changed around them. In the fields in front of them and in the orchard behind, there was no breath of wind. Nothing stirred. There was just the heavy silence pressing in on them, like a nightmare from which they were unable to shake themselves awake.

Yet something happened to Simon and Jenny when they least expected any help. It came in a different form to each of them, but it happened to both of them at the same time.

For Simon, it was as if he felt a touch on his arm. He knew immediately that it was not the Grey Gunner, nor even Jenny. He knew that hand. He remembered when the cloaked figure had come to him in the room on Holkham Hill and had led him away to safety. He had not known at the time that it was the Prince, but he knew now and remembered his words, 'I will be with you always.' Before Simon had time to think of all this and to realise what the touch of that encouraging hand meant, it was gone. But he was left with the feeling of being safe and cared for, even though the danger was still menacingly near.

For Jenny, the same feeling came when, quite unexpectedly, instead of the landscape, shadowed with fear, she saw Andromeda's face, smiling patiently. 'Come on, Jenny,' she seemed to be saying, 'you can do better than this. Where's my fierce panther-fighter?' Her smile faded and Jenny felt herself warmed for a moment in the sympathy which glowed in Andromeda's dark eyes. 'You're not alone, Jenny.' She heard the soft whisper of Andromeda's voice, then the silence fell heavily around her again.

It could have been no more than a second later that the other Grey Gunner came striding towards the gateway, passed through and strode swiftly down the hill without a backward glance. Then suddenly he disappeared. He just vanished. Simon blinked and turned to look at Jenny, who was sitting there open-mouthed.

'What happened?' whispered Jenny. Simon shrugged his shoulders. They were afraid to talk or move because the same thought was at the back of both their minds. What if he was still there but had somehow become invisible? What if *they* couldn't see *him*, but *he* was watching *them*?

'It wouldn't make sense,' Simon said at last, quietly.

'What do you mean?' Jenny frowned.

'He badly wants to capture us and there's no reason at all why he shouldn't if he sees us. So there wouldn't be any point in him turning invisible and watching us.'

Jenny relaxed. 'Probably not.' She looked uneasily over her shoulder. 'But it's not safe here—and now . . .' she glanced at the spot where the Grey Gunner had disappeared, 'it's not safe down there either. What do we do now?'

'What we should have done a long time ago,' said Simon, making a wry face.

'What's that?' asked Jenny, genuinely astonished that there could possibly be any solution to the predicament they were in.

'Ask the King,' stated Simon, simply.

Jenny began to feel hopeful, although she was still completely bemused. 'You mean we should go looking for the King?' she asked hesitantly.

'No,' said Simon. 'Listen. Did you have a feeling just now, as if someone was looking after you?'

'Yes,' said Jenny, conjuring up the picture of Andromeda's smiling face. 'Yes, I did.'

'And remember all the scrapes we've been in, and how something has happened to get us out of them?'

'Yes,' said Jenny again, remembering.

'Well, it seems to me as if we can get in touch with the King and he can say things to us and do things for us, without us actually seeing him face to face.'

Jenny thought this through. 'You're right,' she said. 'Why ever haven't we thought of it before?'

'In fact he probably knows what we're saying and doing right now,' added Simon, 'but I think we still need to ask him.'

Jenny suddenly felt shy of talking to somebody whom she couldn't see. 'Simon,' she said, changing the subject, 'what about your rescue plan?'

Simon felt a little sick, thinking of his simple little rescue plan and the cleverness and cruelty of the Grey Gunners, whom he had completely underestimated. 'Let's just say it's a very good thing we didn't try and put it into action.' He shuddered at the thought of what might have happened when they would inevitably have been caught.

'Right, no more time to waste,' said Simon, glancing swiftly round. He fixed his eyes straight ahead of him and thought of the cloaked figure of the Prince. 'King, your majesty,' he said, 'you know what a fix we're in. We're very grateful for the way you've stopped us getting in even more of a mess. We're sorry that we've been a bit silly and especially sorry that we haven't asked you about things before.'

He paused, then plunged on. 'Well, this is your mission and we're rather stuck. If you want us to rescue Mum and Dad . . .' and here he paused again, a lump in his throat, as he realised what was at stake, 'you'll have to show us exactly what to do next.' Then, as an afterthought, he added, 'Thanks.' He turned to Jenny, slightly embarrassed. 'Well, that's that then.' And they waited.

As they sat, the feeling began growing that they should make their way back to the farmhouse. After what they'd heard, this seemed rather a silly thing to do. So they carried on waiting, hoping something would happen, like the coloured light or the rainbow dove. Time dragged slowly by. No one came and nothing happened. At last Simon said, 'I think we should go back to the farmhouse.'

Jenny looked at him in surprise. 'That's what I've been thinking too,' she said. They smiled at each other, pleased that they had been thinking the same thought. Excited that this must be the King's answer, they were about to get up and move, when they heard the sound of whistling in the orchard. Before they had time to plan what to do, or to fear that the ordeal was about to start all over again, a pair of black boots strode through the gateway and a pair of blue eyes gazed down at them in surprise.

# 9

For a moment Simon and Jenny held the gaze of those bright, blue eyes, their smiles frozen on their faces. Then, despite the slight suspicion that they ought to be on their guard, they both relaxed. There was no mistaking the warmth and interest in those eyes and the hint of a teasing smile about the mouth. One moment he stood there, legs astride, hands on his hips. Then, in one swift movement, he was sitting on the ground beside them, a pleasant-looking boy, just a little older than Simon and Jenny, with a thatch of nut-brown hair. His first words made them both start.

'Jenny and Simon, isn't it?' he said. Jenny and Simon stared back, speechless. The boy grinned broadly, amused at the astonishment on their faces. 'Yes, I thought so,' he went on. 'Don't worry. I'm on your side.' He glanced quickly around him. 'You realise it's not safe here, don't you?' Simon nodded grimly and the boy touched him reassuringly on the shoulder as he stood up. 'Come on. Follow me.' He put a finger to his lips and turned towards the farmhouse.

For the second time, Simon and Jenny made the risky journey across the orchard. It seemed strange that when they thought they were turning away from danger, they had walked right into it. Now it looked as if they were walking back into the worst possible place, but they felt perfectly sure that it was the right thing to do.

The boy led them, not to the garage and kitchen side of the house, but to a small, wooden building at the end of a row of outhouses. It was hardly a room, more the size of a very large cupboard. Simon noted that it was not overlooked by any of the windows in the farmhouse. As for the garage, it was completely out of sight.

When the boy opened the door, Simon and Jenny wrinkled their noses at the awful smell and Jenny hung back for a moment, afraid of what she might find inside that could smell so bad. One look from Simon reminded her of their new resolve to trust the King. No point in trusting when everything looked fine. Trusting meant stepping into dark places sometimes, whatever they smelt like, thought Jenny with a wry smile.

Once inside, the boy closed the door. They were shut in pitch darkness. Jenny stood rigid, with the dreadful stench closing in on her like a huge shapeless monster. She found it hard to breathe, harder still to stop herself from screaming.

She had not made a sound, but she felt a familiar hand take hers and grip it firmly. A second later the room sprang to life in the light of a small oil lamp. Jenny saw the boy's face, bent in concentration as he blew out the match. Simon gave her hand a reassuring squeeze. 'OK?' he asked.

Jenny gulped and nodded. 'Fine,' she said. She looked round her and saw that they were in a kind of small storeroom, evidently being used as a rubbish dump. Apart from a broken box, on which the lantern stood, there was nothing in the room. The pile of rubbish took up most of the space. There was nowhere to sit and not much room to stand.

The boy grinned again. 'Sorry about this. It's not the kind of place to welcome you in, but I can guarantee it's safe. The Grey Gunners don't come near here if they can help it. The Gunner on cleaning duty comes with the rubbish after the evening meal, but otherwise no one comes here at all.'

For a moment the three stood looking at each other.

Now that they had reached a safe place where they could talk, no one really knew where to begin. Simon also wondered how much the boy knew and how much they should tell him of their adventure and their mission.

The first question was obvious. 'How do you know our names?' Simon asked.

His ready smile lit up the boy's face again. 'That's easy,' he said. 'I've heard your mum and dad talk about you.' He held Simon's eyes. 'You look like your dad, don't you?'

Simon smiled back.

The boy arched his eyebrows. 'You don't seem surprised that I've been talking to your mum and dad. Did you know they were here?'

'We saw them through the kitchen window when we first got here,' Simon explained. 'You know more about us than we know about you,' he went on. 'How about telling us one or two things about yourself?'

'Well,' said the boy, 'my name's John and this is my farm.'

'Your farm?' interrupted Jenny, questioningly. 'This old model farm is your farm?'

'That's right,' John looked down and, for the first time since they had met him, the brightness seemed to go out of him. He lifted his eyes and looked at Jenny before he spoke again. She was alarmed to see a look of pain in them and felt ashamed of her blunt question, when she saw how he struggled to control himself before he spoke.

'You don't have to explain,' she said quickly.

'No, it's all right,' said John. He looked down again as he spoke so that his words came quietly. 'The Grey Gunners,' he paused one last time, before continuing in a rush. 'The Grey Gunners came two weeks ago. My father tried to turn them away. They wanted to make our farm a secret base. He couldn't let them do that.'

Simon could see that whatever he had to say next was

hard, so he prompted him. 'He couldn't stop them either, though.'

'No,' said John bleakly, looking up at Simon. 'He tried though. So they killed him.' And here his voice broke, 'And they killed my mother too.'

Jenny put her arm round his shoulders. 'Oh, John,' she said. 'I'm so sorry.'

For a few minutes none of them moved or spoke. Nothing that Simon or Jenny had faced compared with what John had gone through. Jenny thought of the way he had met them and brought them here so cheerfully and she was ashamed of her own complaining and fear. Simon was wondering if he could be so brave, if such an awful thing happened to him. He remembered the words of the Grey Gunner in the orchard. It might happen yet, he thought and shuddered.

John straightened himself and made an attempt to smile. 'Sorry about that,' he said in the same matter of fact way he had apologised for the smelly room they were in.

Simon and Jenny began speaking at the same time. They stopped and waited for each other.

'Go on, Simon,' said Jenny.

'Do Mum and Dad know about all this?' asked Simon. 'Have you managed to speak to them?'

'Yes, they know. I've had to fool the Gunners—at least I hope I have—into thinking that my mind has been affected by what's happened and they're not too worried about letting me move about freely. But I have to be careful and I've only had the chance to speak with your mum and dad twice—no, three times. But that's been enough for us to put each other in the picture.'

Simon nodded. 'What did you want to say, Jenny?'

'Oh.' Jenny looked at Simon, wondering if she really ought to ask her question. 'I just wondered,' she began hesitantly, 'if you . . .' Both boys waited expectantly as she struggled for the next words, 'were a follower of the

King?' she plunged on, then stopped, looking embarrassed. Simon looked uncomfortably from Jenny to John. John said nothing. Then he leaned forward and, in the circle of light thrown by the lantern, he drew something in the dust on the box. Simon looked puzzled and John, seeing his look, hastily wiped it away. Jenny touched John's arm. 'I know what that was. You are a follower of the King, aren't you?' she said confidently to John. Then to Simon she explained, 'That was the sign Andromeda made. I recognised it.'

John was wary now. 'What do you know of the King?' he asked. Jenny opened her mouth to explain.

'No,' Simon said. 'Jenny, be careful.' She understood what he meant, but she was sure, as sure as if it had been Andromeda standing with them.

'The King has put power over everything . . .' began Jenny, her gaze steadily on John. Simon gasped, horrified and was about to interrupt when John's voice, with a hint of laughter in it, continued, 'in the hands of the Prince.' Then both he and Jenny laughed for joy. Simon's mouth dropped open in amazement. Then he too smiled as the old, warm feeling of joy crept over him. He clasped John's hand. How incredible. This was the answer to his plea for help. The King had John here all along. He had only been waiting for Simon and Jenny to be ready.

Then it all came out. John told them how the King had helped him when he had felt so sad and angry that he had wanted to give up hope. He told them of how their parents had been brought to the farmhouse and how the King had given him three short opportunities to speak to them. Finally he told them of the feeling that he had had when he woke that morning, that today something would begin, for which he had been waiting. It was that strange feeling that had taken him out to the orchard at a time he would normally have been in the fields. 'But I was still surprised when I found you there,' he said, smiling at Simon and Jenny.

Then Simon and Jenny told their story; from the arrival of Michael and Andromeda to the Grey Gunner disappearing into thin air. They explained the mission that the King had given them and how they felt that the next step was to rescue their parents.

John rubbed his chin thoughtfully. 'I'll have to think,' he said. 'Meantime, I'll have to smuggle you out something to eat or you'll be no good to the King or anybody.'

'We have got some of the food left that Michael gave us.' said Jenny, wrinkling her nose. 'Though I don't quite feel like eating anything at the moment.'

'We'll have to stay here, will we?' asked Simon.

'Yes, I'm afraid so,' said John regretfully. 'You're safe here till after the evening meal tonight. We'll have to think of something before then.'

'John,' asked Jenny, 'why did the Grey Gunner we saw suddenly disappear?'

'Ah, yes,' smiled John. 'You must have had a shock when that happened. Perhaps it's a good thing you hadn't seen it before. It might have given you a few nightmares along the journey.'

Simon and Jenny looked at each other. 'Whatever was it?' asked Simon.

'Transplacement,' stated John.

'Transwhat?' asked Simon.

'Transplacement. It's one of the nice little tricks the Grey Gunners have. They can travel from one place to another within a limited area. Happily they can't do it too often here because it needs a greater supply of power than we have on our planet. In fact it's forbidden unless it's by strict order of the Old Ruler or one of the Generals.'

'So we shouldn't have really seen it happen?'

'No, he shouldn't have done it. I can guess who that was. Grendra, one of the high-ups from the ZX Division.

He's a law to himself. But he's one of the Old Ruler's top men so he can get away with it. In fact he was one of . . .' He stopped, lifted his shoulders and sighed deeply.

'One of those who killed your parents?' put in Jenny softly.

'He gave the orders. Listen, I must go,' John said, brusquely. 'I'll be back as soon as I can.' He slipped quickly out of the room, leaving Jenny and Simon alone with the dim light of the lantern and the nauseating smell of the rubbish for company. But oddly enough, they felt happy with the turn things had now taken.

It took the scream from the yard outside to bring back a fleeting feeling of the old fear and panic. One single scream and then silence. They looked at each other in dismay. Now what should they do? Wait here as John had told them? If something had happened to John, they would wait for ever. Dare they go outside and investigate? If they did, would they walk straight into the Grey Gunners?

# 10

Simon strained to hear any sounds from the yard outside. Jenny stood silently behind him, her ear pressed against the thick wood of the door. Simon thought he could pick up a faint noise, the kind of rubbing sound his arm would make if he pulled it across the door. No, not rubbing; dragging, that's what it was. Something being dragged along—or someone.

He pictured John unconscious, or worse, being dragged across the yard by the Grey Gunners. Should he go out? What should he do? A moment ago he had felt so sure everything was in the King's control. Now, he just didn't know. 'What do I do now?' he asked silently. 'Please help me to do the right thing.'

He jumped as there was an explosion of sound in the yard outside. He had no more idea of what was happening than when there had been only silence. There was a scream, followed by voices shouting and footsteps running. Whatever was happening? Simon felt he could hardly bear waiting behind the door a moment longer. His hand was almost on the knob when the voices and footsteps began to grow fainter until there was only the silence again.

Jenny was very glad of the light from the lamp. Despite the smell, which she was almost getting used to, she felt safe inside their cupboard-sized room. She had the feeling that the King had led them to this hiding-place in the nick of time and whatever was going on outside, they were not meant to be part of it; not yet.

She had moved away from the door when there was the

sound of footsteps suddenly just outside and the door was thrust open. As the door swung open, it knocked Simon back against her, so that they both nearly fell and upset the lamp. Jenny put her hand out to the wall to regain her balance. It was not the way she had imagined she would make her first face to face encounter with a Grey Gunner, caught completely off guard like this—and trapped.

But it was not a Grey Gunner she saw when she straightened up. It was John. There was no time to feel relief. Jenny saw John's face briefly in the lamplight and he looked tense.

'I've just knocked Lasky out,' he said shortly. He leaned against the door, breathing hard.

Simon and Jenny stared at him, not knowing what to say. 'I've dragged him into the barn out of sight,' John went on, struggling for control. 'But it won't take them long to find him once they miss him and start searching. Then they'll begin looking for whoever knocked him out.' He grimaced. 'Sorry. It was a stupid thing to do. I'm afraid it means we'll have to get out of here as fast as we can.'

Jenny wished she could think of something reassuring to say but she had caught the sense of panic behind John's words.

Simon's mouth was dry as he touched John's arm. 'Is there something you're not telling us? We heard a scream and a lot of noise out there.'

John glanced quickly at Jenny. 'I suppose you'd better know the whole story. It was your mum and dad. I don't know how they'd got as far as the yard, but they were trying to escape. I'd just gone into the barn to check the landrover when I heard them cross the yard. A couple of Malek's men must have been on duty at the corner of the cowshed because they suddenly appeared from nowhere and grabbed your mum. When she screamed your dad stopped and turned, but by then they had injected her with something and were dragging her away. Your dad saw Lasky before I did. He had his laser gun pointed at your dad, but had his back to me as he crossed the doorway of the barn. I think I acted on reflex when I knocked him out. I'd only just dragged him inside the barn when more Grey Gunners came running into the yard.'

'And Dad?' asked Jenny anxiously.

'He was crossing to the barn when he heard them coming. He deliberately turned and walked to meet them,' stated John.

'Good for you, Dad!' said Simon proudly.

They were all quiet for a moment, thinking of what had just happened. Then John opened the door a crack and peered cautiously into the yard. 'Come on,' he said quietly, turning to the others. 'We must go now, while we can.'

John stepped out into the deserted yard and Simon followed, narrowing his eyes against the fierceness of the light. Simon jumped as the silence was broken by the sound of mocking laughter from the barn. Out of the shadowed doorway stepped a Grey Gunner, laughing as he rubbed his head gingerly. As if that had been a prearranged signal, from the doorways and from behind corners appeared half a dozen more Grey Gunners, levelling their laser guns at the shed.

Without thinking if it was the best thing to do, Simon pulled John back into the shed and slammed the door shut.

To gain what little time they could, Simon and John barricaded the door. There was not much in the shed, which was worth putting across it. An old piece of piping was the best find. It fitted diagonally across the door, like a gigantic bar. It took the Grey Gunners a few minutes to break the door down. In the end they used their laser guns and sliced through the piping as easily as if it had been a piece of paper. But the delay gave John and Simon just enough time to do one very important thing: to hide Jenny under the rubbish. The piping clattered to the floor and the debris, which they had piled against the door, scattered as the door burst open. Three Grey Gunners stood framed in the doorway, their laser guns pointing at John.

Simon, standing behind John and to one side, could hardly believe that, after all their narrow escapes, they were trapped at last. Remembering Holkham Hill, he half expected the cloaked figure of the Prince to appear, paralyse the Grey Gunners and rescue them all.

For a few seconds they stood quite still, Simon and John meeting the cold gaze of the three Grey Gunners. Simon felt a strange dizziness as if all of this was unreal, a nightmare from which he would suddenly wake up. Then the tallest of the Grey Gunners stepped forward and spoke. His voice and words chilled Simon.

'So, we have you at last, Simon Miller. You have caused us a lot of trouble.' His eyes narrowed and the smile vanished. 'A lot of trouble,' he repeated harshly. 'But not for much longer.' Simon knew that voice. He had heard it making threats once before. The memory made him shudder.

'It seems John has been playing a little game with us, Commander,' broke in the Grey Gunner that John had knocked out. John remained silent, which seemed to amuse the leader of the party.

'Indeed it does, Lasky,' he said. 'Now we shall join the game shall we, John? Shall we find out exactly what it does take to make a mind break?'

Simon and John were prodded out into the yard. Lasky glanced back at the shed. 'What about the girl?' he asked, touching Grendra's arm. 'She's sure to be with them. Aren't you going to search the shed?'

'The shed?' replied Grendra coolly, as he walked on. 'As you saw, there was only rubbish in the shed. Actually, I though the stench in the shed was rather bad. We ought to do something about it. A hazard to our health, wouldn't you say? Rennad, Cordul,' he called and two Grey Gunners came running. 'Burn that small shed down, will you—but make sure the fire doesn't spread to the outhouses.'

It took all of Simon's will-power not to look at John. John had still said nothing, not even with this new dreadful crisis facing them. Simon struggled not to let his fear show on his face. Jenny was still hidden under the rubbish in the shed. Surely it would be better to tell them and let her be caught than let her be burnt alive. Unless John had some plan. If he had, Simon dare not let him down. But if he hadn't . . . Simon gulped and tried to think calmly. If only the Prince was here.

They were at the farmhouse now. A Grey Gunner pushed the door open and motioned them in. As they stepped over the threshold, a feeling of peace settled over Simon. 'Power over everything is in the hands of the Prince.' The thought grew suddenly inside him.

'Be with Jenny. Help her,' he pleaded silently. 'Don't let her be frightened. Don't let her die.'

Then he tensed as Grendra strode past him, calling out 'Bring the Millers here at once, will you?' In the long moment that followed, as he waited for his parents' appearance, Simon caught the faint whiff of smoke from across the yard.

# 11

From the moment the Grey Gunners had burst in through the door and there was nothing more he could do, John had concentrated on talking silently to the King. He felt almost as if he was sending his unspoken thoughts into a long, dark, empty tunnel, where no one was listening. It even seemed as if there was another voice, close at hand, which threatened to be stronger than his own. 'Give up. Give in,' it said. 'There's no King. He wouldn't have let you get in a jam like this. Better give the Grey Gunners the help they need and help yourself by doing it. Tell them about Jenny. Don't waste any more time. Come on, John.'

While this struggle was going on inside, John was also aware of what was going on around him, as if he was watching a play, but couldn't quite get the hang of the plot. He saw the Millers come in. Mr Miller looked tired and strained. Mrs Miller looked dazed and had to be half carried in, then propped up in a chair.

'Dad,' said Simon with a catch in his voice, and rushed into his father's arms.

John was aware of the faint smell of smoke in the background. Suddenly his head cleared and he had the same feeling of closeness to the King he had had after his parents had been killed. His thoughts focussed on one thing: 'Please help Jenny. Please look after her.' He looked round the room. Grendra and Lasky were watching the Millers closely. John saw light come into Mrs Miller's eyes as she became aware that it was Simon kneeling in front of her, holding her hand. Mr Miller stood by her chair, supporting her. 'Please look after us all,' John added.

John became aware that the Grey Gunners had closed round the Millers in a semicircle, pointing their laser guns at them. Grendra stood close to John. 'I don't suppose you feel inclined to tell us where the girl is?' he said. John looked at the laser guns and inhaled the odour of smoke. It seemed he no longer had any choice.

He was about to speak when he heard again what he had heard earlier, when he had made his plea to the King. He thought then that he had imagined a faint rumble in the distance. Now it came again distinctly. The next moment the scene was lit, for a split second, in a bright silver light. Then they were all plunged into darkness, and a loud roar shook the walls of the farmhouse. Immediately afterwards the room was filled with a heavy silence, while outside there was the sound of torrential rain.

It was the house where he had grown up and John knew every corner and brick of it. He also knew the Grey Gunners and what they would do. There was no time for hesitation. He must act quickly.

Lasky was shouting, 'Don't let them get away,' while Grendra, his voice calmer and more forceful, called out, 'Hold Miller and the boy.'

John edged his way slowly backwards in the darkness, trying to remember the layout of the furniture and the positioning of the Grey Gunners before the next flash of lightning lit the room. He was making for the kitchen doorway.

He stopped as a beam of yellow light swung round the room, caught him and dazzled his eyes. Soon the room was lit by the pale glow of the torches of the Grey Gunners.

'Leaving us, John?' came Grendra's mocking voice. John felt his spirits sink. He had been so sure that the King was providing the means for their escape. It seemed impossible to get away from the Grey Gunners.

Grendra indicated with his torch beam that John move to join the Millers. For the first time since leaving the shed, John's eyes met Simon's and he was surprised to see the glow of excitement in them. He raised his eyebrows questioningly.

Lasky pushed John to the other side of Mrs Miller. 'We're wasting time,' he said. 'Let's get on with it.'

'It would be easier to get it over with, of course.' Grendra drummed his fingers on the table in front of him. His voice when he spoke was deliberately calm. 'But we need the girl.'

'But I thought the girl was in the . . .'

'Probably,' interrupted Grendra. 'But we keep them alive until we're sure. In the meantime we can . . .'

But they never discovered his plans for the storm was now directly overhead and the next flash of lightning scorched through the room where they were standing, striking the edge of the table behind which Grendra was standing. The roll of thunder drowned the frightened shouts of the Grey Gunners, as a wall of flame shot up in front of them. It left John and the Millers alone on the other side of the flames, with the door only a few yards away.

It took them only seconds to open the door and, with Mr Miller supporting his wife, they stumbled out into the yard. They pulled up quickly as lightning again flashed across the yard within a few feet of them.

Suddenly, the rainswept scene in front of them came to life in a flickering orange glow. They were near the barn, the deserted yard in front of them and the outhouses empty and ghostly in the dark. Simon raced across the yard, only to stop again, frozen with fear, as the light from the burning farmhouse showed clearly the blackened outline of the half-burnt shed.

'Jenny!' he yelled into the rain. A figure stepped out of the outhouses.

'Simon, I'm here.' Jenny ran towards him.

Together they raced to the barn. John was already ahead of them, leaping into the landrover, when there was a faint moan from behind them and Mrs Miller collapsed on to the cobblestones.

'Carry on,' called Mr Miller into the driving rain. 'I'll bring her.' He lifted the crumpled figure and ran, stumbling across the yard as John reversed the landrover out of the barn.

'Couldn't we do with a land-speeder now!' said John wryly as the engine stalled.

Mr Miller lifted his wife into the landrover to Jenny and Simon's waiting hands. They all cast an anxious backward glance toward the farmhouse. The yard was full of shadows and they knew how quickly and silently the Grey Gunners could move under cover of darkness. The engine roared to life and they gave up straining to hear any sound of pursuit. But as they moved off into the night, they could not be absolutely sure that the Grey Gunners were not following, unseen and unheard.

As they drove along they began to relax and Mrs Miller recovered consciousness. Mr Miller began his story, telling them how he had been captured as he was leaving the Defence Plant and how he had been brought to the farmhouse to join his wife. At first the Grey Gunners had seemed very considerate and patient. It was only later that he began to see what they were really like.

'I can't understand what they are up to,' he said, his eyes concentrating on the dark, winding road ahead. 'Everything they are doing seems to be very secretive. It's as if they are waiting for something—or someone.'

Simon and Jenny exchanged glances. 'Yes, I wondered that too,' Mrs Miller joined in. 'I wondered if . . .' Then she fell silent.

'What?' prompted Simon. 'What did you wonder?'

'You tell us what happened to you,' said Mrs Miller, changing the subject.

Between them, Jenny and Simon told their story, drawing gasps of alarm from Mrs Miller as they described one narrow escape after another. When they had finished there was a long moment of silence. Mrs Miller shook her head. 'I don't quite know what to say.' She smiled down at Jenny, hugging her to her. 'It sounds incredible.'

'Yes, it does,' said Mr Miller quietly from the driving seat. 'I'm proud of you both for the way you've faced the Grey Gunners. But I . . .' He stopped, struggling for the right words.

'Go on, Dad,' encouraged Simon, leaning forward.

'Simon, I'm afraid I can't think of a good way of putting it. I wish I didn't have to say this to you. But we need to know exactly what it is we're up against, if we're to be ready to deal with the Grey Gunners. Simon, Jenny, I know that you won't quite see things this way, but I'm afraid you'll have to face up to the truth sooner or later. The fact is that there isn't really a King, or a Prince either. It would be nice to think there was. The Old Ruler isn't as bad as you make him out to be. It's just the Grey Gunners of Gehalla we're up against.'

Simon and Jenny were shocked. They sat on the edge of their seats, waiting open-mouthed to protest. John sat grimly in his seat next to Mrs Miller.

'No, don't try and argue with me,' Mr Miller went on. 'I know you think I'm wrong. But it's important that you face up to things as they really are. No one's going to help us fight the Grey Gunners. We have to do it ourselves.'

After that there was a complete and heavy silence in the landrover. Eventually Mrs Miller leaned forward. 'Where are we going, John?' she asked.

'I believe Mr Miller has an idea,' John answered quietly.

'Yes,' Mr Miller agreed. 'Now that John's got us back

on the main road, I've realised it's not far from here to Greg Farnham's. He lives in a fairly quiet spot near the border. He'll give us shelter, not to mention breakfast. Even if he's gone, I think his house will be pretty safe. The Gunners have better things to do than to guard empty houses.'

'Unless they know that someone is coming there,' thought John. Maybe what he had gone through at the farm was making him too suspicious. He decided to say nothing.

It was nearly morning when they reached their destination. It was a beautiful house, even with only the dark blue light of dawn to view it by. It stood well back from the roadside, a long gravel path leading up to it. Hedges marked the boundaries of the wide front lawns. It looked both peaceful and inviting as they walked up to it, leaving the landrover in the long grass at the roadside.

There had been a short discussion as to whether it would be wiser for just one or two to investigate or for all of them to go. They decided that if it was a trap, they would be no safer in the landrover than in the house. It would be better for them all to stick together.

Mr Miller decided against ringing the doorbell or calling out. There was an air of emptiness about the house. They all stood huddled in the shadows of the front porch as Mr Miller fiddled with the lock.

'Amazing what you pick up at the Defence Plant,' he whispered, swinging the door open. They paused in the large hall. Straight ahead a wide, central staircase wound up to the first floor landing. A door opened off to the left and two to the right.

Mr Miller motioned to the others as he paused by a door, which was slightly ajar. Gingerly, he pushed it open. The cold, early morning light showed the shadowy shapes of tables, a settee and high wing-backed chairs. Jenny was feeling for the light switch when Mr Miller's hand closed over hers. He shook his head and advanced quietly into the room.

Jenny and Mrs Miller, with John just behind them, stood blinking, dazzled in the doorway, when the light went on. Mr Miller was standing half-way between the doorway and the chair at the moment when a hand reached out and switched on the large table lamp. In its light they saw Lasky, leaning against the far wall by the window, smiling at them. A head peered round the wing of the chair. Simon felt almost relieved when he recognised Grendra. So now they knew the worst. All Grendra could do, it seemed, was to lie in wait for them. Though however he knew . . .?

There Simon's thoughts stopped abruptly and he froze in horror. Moving slowly out of the shadows on the far side of the room came a tall figure dressed in green and grey with highlights of silver, making him gleam in an unearthly way as he moved. Simon had never seen him before, but he felt a cold, clammy fear as he looked up into the steely grey eyes set in that proud face. The grey eyes seemed to pierce him through. Then they moved slowly over Jenny's face and back again to Simon.

'Simon and Jenny,' said the deep, melodious voice, 'I am so glad you have come.' His mouth twisted into a cold, cruel smile, which added menace to his words. 'I have been looking forward to meeting you,' said the Old Ruler.

# 12

While he spoke everyone stood perfectly still, as if a spell had been cast over them. John, who was still in the doorway, could possibly have slipped quietly out of sight and attempted to escape. But he knew, quite sensibly, it was no use thinking of any such thing.

All eyes were fixed on the face of the Old Ruler. He was much younger than Simon had expected, probably not much older than Michael. Despite his stern features and his cold gaze, there was something about him which drew you to him. Despite themselves, they all stood there dumbfounded.

The Old Ruler had hardly taken his eyes off Simon's face. 'You know me, don't you, Simon?' he said softly. Simon merely stared back. A strange light feeling flooded through him. He felt as if he could let go the cares and anxieties of the last few weeks. There was no need to worry about the way his father felt any more. Now he could relax and let go. This tall, glittering figure in grey and green was here now. He was strong. His voice was firm and deep. All Simon had to do was to listen to him.

From a long way off, Simon heard another voice. It was angry and loud. He felt annoyed. He wished this new, harsh voice would be quiet. A figure pushed his way in front of him, so that it blocked him from the Old Ruler's gaze. As John strode forward, the others began to stir and move too. Simon felt as if someone had dropped him from a warm, sunny height to a cold, dark chasm.

'Yes, I know you,' John was saying. 'I have never seen your face before because it has been such a closely guarded secret. You have many disguises and, though you have tricked the whole world into believing you are wise and good, you have many dark and dangerous forms. I know you, your majesty Gar-Zelubal, high master of our planet, chief of our leaders, commander of our armies, the Old Ruler himself.'

As he finished, Jenny let out a gasp and held on to Mrs Miller's arm. She was alarmed, both at finding themselves in the clutches of their arch-enemy, and at seeing John suddenly crumple to the ground, merely because the Old Ruler pointed his hand towards him.

'So, his power within you is greater than I thought,' said Grendra, looking at the still form of John, stretched out at his feet.

The situation looked pretty grim, especially for John. But if John had not acted when he did, Simon might have been lost. Caught completely off his guard, his mind had almost slipped under the total control of the Old Ruler.

Simon was completely himself again as he knelt down beside John. He looked up at the inscrutable face of the Old Ruler. Gar-Zelubal was still smiling, but Simon was able to recognise now the hidden anger in the depth of his eyes.

Jenny felt at that moment, watching her brother calmly facing their enemy, that she and her parents could quite possibly have walked out of the room and no one would have tried to stop them. The battle was quite clearly between the Old Ruler and Simon. She avoided looking at Grendra and Lasky and tried to calm her thoughts. She wondered, for the first time, if the Old Ruler and the Grey Gunners were able to read thoughts. She decided that even if they could, she had to try it anyway. She focussed her mind on the King and she asked as clearly and as urgently as she could, for his help.

'You probably know about this, what a bad fix we are in now. There's nothing we can do and there's no one else to help, so please can you do something. Please help Si . . .'

Here she stopped abruptly as the Old Ruler turned his eyes away from Simon and stared coldly at her. He was beside her in one swift stride and grasped her arm so tightly that she gave a small cry of pain.

'Stop it!' he said harshly, all the charm and melody gone from his voice. 'You little fool, don't you know when you're beaten?'

'You stop it,' cut in Mr Miller, trying to pull the Old Ruler's arm away from Jenny. 'Leave my daughter alone.'

Jenny looked calmly into the Old Ruler's eyes. He was so angry that she felt a tingle of excitement. It must mean that she had frightened him with her plea to the King. It must mean that the King's power was greater than his.

Lasky walked over to Mr Miller and pushed him down on the settee. He stood behind him, laser gun dangling casually from his hand. 'Take it easy, Mr Miller. Everything's under control,' he said.

Abruptly the Old Ruler let go of Jenny and walked swiftly over to Grendra. He whispered a few sharp words in his ear, turned and strode out of the room. Grendra immediately got up to follow him.

Four Grey Gunners entered the room and took positions where they could watch the prisoners, laser guns at the ready. Jenny and Simon exchanged glances across the room. The Old Ruler certainly wasn't taking any chances. He must really be worried about something.

'Look here,' burst out Mr Miller, 'what is going on? You seem to be spending an incredible amount of time chasing a red herring. I haven't got any information to pass on to you. My wife knows nothing of my work. As for the children, surely you could let them go.'

Whatever he had expected Lasky's reaction to be, Mr Miller was taken by surprise. Lasky leaned for support on the back of the settee and began to laugh.

'My dear Mr Miller,' he said at last, trying to control himself. 'Are you trying to tell us not to waste our time?'

He glanced at the other Grey Gunners to see if they had shared the joke. 'Don't you think Mr Miller is being very thoughtful?' Then, as the Old Ruler re-entered the room he turned to him. 'Your majesty, Mr Miller would like us to release his children.'

The Old Ruler did not smile. He glanced briefly at Mr Miller. 'I agree with Mr Miller. These games have gone on long enough. We are all now very bored with playing hide and seek. We will certainly let the children go—when they have told us what we want to know. Mrs Miller, I will leave you here with your son and daughter for a few minutes. See if you can persuade them to tell us where we can find the Prince. Meanwhile, I have some electronic experiments in which Mr Miller will be interested.'

Two of the Gunners marched Mr Miller out of the room, following Grendra. The Old Ruler paused behind them in the doorway. 'Bring the boy,' he called over his shoulder. The remaining two Gunners picked up John's limp body. Finally Lasky followed them to the door. He turned to look at Simon and Jenny. He shook his head and laughed. Then he closed the door and the three of them were left alone.

They waited for a few moments, listening to the sound of retreating footsteps. Somewhere in the distance, they heard the slam of a closing door. Then there was silence.

'What's all this about the Prince?' asked Mrs Miller.

'What Prince?' returned Simon. His eyes met Jenny's puzzled gaze. 'Are we being bugged?' he mouthed and let his eyes rove round the room, as if searching for something.

Jenny understood and nodded vigorously. She turned questioningly to her mother. Mrs Miller had grasped the potential problem and took charge of the situation. She winked at Jenny and then she said in exasperated tones, 'Well, I can see that neither of you is going to talk.

That's quite obvious. But think about your father. Goodness knows what they're doing to him.'

'Don't you think we'd tell them if we knew where the Prince was?' Simon was saying, when the door burst open.

'No,' said the Old Ruler in a chilling voice. 'I don't think you would.' Behind him stood Grendra and two Grey Gunners. 'You obviously have not the sense to talk when it is necessary. We have wasted enough time. Mrs Miller, we will see if there is another way you can be used to persuade them to talk.' Grendra strode over to her and roughly pinioned her arms behind her back.

'Bring her here, Grendra,' the cold voice went on.

Mrs Miller winced with pain and Jenny flung herself at Grendra, beating him with her fists. 'Leave my mother alone. Don't you dare hurt her.'

Simon, who was looking at the Old Ruler just then to see his reaction, was the first to see the strange, new thing. Behind the Old Ruler and the two Grey Gunners, there was a flash of light in the dim hall. It flashed gold and blue, orange, red and green. Finally it settled to a dazzling white, flecked through with tints of all the colours it had shown. It had grown so bright that Simon was forced to look away. But, as he averted his eyes, he glimpsed the outline of a person in the light.

The Old Ruler had been looking at Jenny. So it was not because he followed Simon's gaze that the Old Ruler suddenly spun round. It was because he sensed some force, in conflict with his own.

All that followed happened so quickly, that it was only in piecing it together afterwards, that the Millers realised what they had seen. A flash of white light streaked past the Old Ruler, knocking him off balance. It made straight for Grendra, so that he fell backwards, releasing Mrs Miller as he did so.

Simon and Jenny were amazed to see Grendra pinioned

to the ground by a snow-white leopard. Simon dived to pick up the laser gun, which had clattered to the ground just beyond Grendra's reach.

The Old Ruler was levelling his gun at the leopard when a tall figure in blue and gold moved up swiftly behind him. A second person, in identical dress, covered the two Grey Gunners.

Jenny and Mrs Miller had been standing quite stunned at the turn events were taking. Now Jenny, looking out into the hall, let out a sudden cry of delight. 'Andromeda!' she called. They all turned in the direction of her gaze. And there, sure enough, was Andromeda.

It was only a second or two, but long enough for the Old Ruler to draw a small, metal object from his tunic and send it spinning through the air. Michael, standing with his laser gun pointed at the Old Ruler's back, could not possibly have reacted fast enough to stop it.

It found its mark. A pitiful cry of pain came from the wounded leopard as the red blood spurted down its side. One moment the large cat lay moaning in a pool of shimmering light. The next, there lay Grendra on the ground and next to him, the small, still form of a black and brown cat.

# 13

'Alabaster,' cried Jenny, running over to the furry bundle. Andromeda moved quickly into the room. She stopped stock still as, in one swift move, Grendra eased himself up, grabbed Jenny's arm and pointed his laser gun in her ribs. 'Release him,' he said to Michael, 'or the girl dies.'

For a moment there was complete stillness in the room. The hope and excitement of the last few minutes died as suddenly as they had come. The Old Ruler did not wait to see Michael's reaction. He merely walked out of the range of the laser. He paused in front of Grendra and Jenny, who had risen to their feet.

He was looking at the pitiful form of Alabaster as he smiled and said scornfully, 'So this is the terrifying extent of the power of the Prince.' He laughed as if he were no longer afraid of anything Simon or Jenny or the others could do. There was no doubt that the power of the Old Ruler was very great. He was clever and he was cruel. It seemed that he could not fail to win.

But it was just at that point that he made the one mistake he really should not have made. In his delight at the helplessness of his enemies, he forgot how strong love can be and how it can overcome fear. So he laughed. 'A cat,' he said scornfully and he kicked the helpless, wounded ball of fur that was Alabaster.

Jenny had been feeling a horrible ache of emptiness and helplessness. She realised that it was her fault that Alabaster had been hurt and that, just when it looked as if they had the enemy cornered, the tables had been turned. If only she had thought before she called out and before she moved.

But when the Old Ruler laughed and kicked her beloved Alabaster, all these feelings vanished. Instead of the all-powerful Old Ruler, she saw a mean bully, who should not be allowed to get away with what he had just done.

Simon, who had always got the better of Jenny in any of their childhood fights, stood open-mouthed with amazement when he saw how accurately she thrust her elbow into Grendra's stomach so that he doubled up in pain and dropped his laser gun. Before they had all recovered from the surprise, Jenny had kicked the Old Ruler in the shins and scooped up the limp body of Alabaster. 'You bully,' she cried, and without meaning to, put her foot down on the fallen laser gun.

Michael and Simon had wasted no time in recapturing the Old Ruler. Andromeda had moved quickly to Grendra's side, covering him with a strange weapon Jenny had not seen before. 'Well done, Jenny,' she said and smiled the old, familiar smile that had cheered Jenny through many a crisis.

Looking past her, Jenny noticed half a dozen or so people dressed similarly to Andromeda and Michael, who had been standing out in the hall. Four of them disappeared in different directions, but two came into the room and secured Grendra, the Old Ruler and the two Grey Gunners with some thin chains of amber metal, that must have been much stronger than they looked.

Both Grendra and the Old Ruler were strangely silent until the chains had been fixed. It was clear that they were controlling their anger by an effort of will. Simon thought that it must be a policy that the Old Ruler had enforced, that they were to react to capture without resistance and without emotion.

It was not until Michael spoke to him that the Old Ruler lifted his eyes, blazing with anger.

'You realise that it cannot be long now before the end?' asked Michael. The Old Ruler looked not at Michael but at Jenny.

'Your father,' he said harshly, none of the milky smoothness left in his voice now. 'Did you think it was more important to save a cat than your father?'

Jenny went crimson with shame. She had thought only of Alabaster. She had failed again. She should have remembered that her father's life, and John's too, was in danger. Then she felt the warm bundle stir in her arms. She stroked the matted fur and held him to her face. Two slow tears trickled down her face and on to his back.

'Don't listen to him, Jenny,' said Andromeda, putting her arm round Jenny's shoulders. 'Don't you know by now that he takes a little of the truth and twists it? He knows exactly how and where to hurt. But,' she added, smiling, 'he sometimes underestimates our strength. He didn't know how strong love could make you, Jenny.'

The Old Ruler wasted no time. He turned then to Mrs Miller. 'You are perhaps the only one left, who can do anything to rescue your husband from his fate. You are older than the others, wiser. Talk to them. Tell them they must let me go, because if the guards in the Treatment Room pick up signals on the monitor of my capture, they will begin systematically programming Mr Miller. Better for him, I believe, but you would probably prefer him as he is now. Mrs Miller, I appeal to you.'

Complete bewilderment showed in Mrs Miller's face. She examined the Old Ruler's face, a mask of patient concern. She turned to Jenny and Andromeda.

'Don't believe him, Mummy. He's lying,' burst out Simon.

Mrs Miller shook her head. 'I don't know. I really don't know.'

'Mrs Miller, there is not much time,' broke in the Old Ruler urgently.

'She is not the oldest,' interrupted a voice unexpectedly. 'I am.'

Everyone turned, drawn by the quiet authority in Michael's voice. 'I am the oldest in this room,' he went on. 'I am older than you, Old Ruler. My home is not this planet or Gehalla. It is the Star of the Prince, for I am a servant and a friend of the Prince, a Commander in his army and a member of his Council. Why I am here is the business only of the Prince. I have come commissioned by the King and Andromeda comes with me, endowed with power as I am.'

He turned to Mrs Miller. 'Simon and Jenny, for reasons which I cannot explain to you now, have been chosen by the King for this special mission. I believe they have told you much of what has befallen them. It was hoped that you and your husband would join them on the next stage of their mission. They have done well.' Here he paused to smile at Simon and Jenny. 'They have done very well. But much of the battle is fought here,' he continued, touching his head, 'in the mind and in the heart. You are faced now with a conflict of your own. You must decide who you are going to believe. You must decide alone.'

Because of the complete silence in the room, as all eyes turned on Mrs Miller, they all became aware of a faint sound from another part of the house. A sharp cry of pain was followed by a short silence. Next came moans, a prolonged whimpering and then silence again.

Mrs Miller turned to Michael. 'What can we do?'

Before answering, Michael stepped up to Mrs Miller and clasped her hands. Smiling down at her, he said, 'Good. You will never regret it.' Simon came to her side and squeezed her arm. 'Good for you, Mum,' he said.

'And now,' said Michael, 'we must act quickly. There is no time to be lost.'

'What about Alabaster?' put in Jenny anxiously.

'Yes, Alabaster first,' said Michael, taking the cat gently from Jenny. 'Andromeda?' he queried.

Andromeda took a small bottle of violet liquid from a pocket in her golden belt. She dabbed a little of it round the wound. 'I'm sorry, my precious,' she said, 'you should have had this long before now. Sleep now and let the ointment do its healing work, my brave friend.'

'He'll be all right?' asked Jenny.

'We'll have to wait and see,' answered Andromeda, taking him from Michael. 'The wounds caused by the Old Ruler can be deep, but the Prince has the power to heal them completely.' She bent and kissed the small, furry head.

'Come,' said Michael, 'we must hurry. First we must find Mr Miller and John.' Michael turned to the door, Simon hard on his heels. The others were following in the rear, when the Old Ruler played his last and most unexpected trick. Jenny saw him lift his chained hands high in the air. She cried out because she thought he was going to strike Simon. But even as Simon turned, the hands were no longer there. The Old Ruler simply vanished.

Immediately Michael called out 'Alexon!' and one of his two companions leapt forward and grasped both of Grendra's hands. 'I don't think you could manage to do it anyway, Grendra,' said Michael. 'But we can't take any risks. We don't want to lose both of you before we've had a proper chance to talk. Now let's go.'

They crossed the hall silently. They were almost at the darkened doorway of the room opposite when there was the sound of footsteps on the upstairs landing. Michael motioned them into the shadows of the stairwell and they waited as the footsteps drew nearer. Grendra stood motionless in Michael's firm grip, though he grimaced as Michael clamped his hand over his mouth. Suddenly one of the other Grey Gunners struggled out of the grasp of Michael's Companion and yelled out a warning. They secured him again immediately, but the footsteps had stopped.

Simon wondered if they should all rush out and up the

stairs, when the footsteps began again, this time running down the steps towards them. Two figures suddenly bounded over the banister at the foot of the stairs. At the same time, two others came hurtling over the top rail of the landing into their midst, making Michael release his hold on Grendra. But all was well, for it was on top of Grendra that one of the figures landed. It was John! Picking himself up, John levelled his laser gun at Michael, then lowered it in surprise, as he recognised the uniform; for with him had come two of Michael's Companions and Mr Miller.

For a moment everyone was speechless. Then they all began talking at once. There was a great deal of laughter, exclamations of delight and introductions.

'Next time use your radio, will you!' said Michael to one of the Companions. 'Now, Mr Miller, will you tell us exactly what has happened?'

Mr Miller looked at Simon and Jenny for a long minute before answering. 'I've got an apology to make to you two. John and I were in a pretty bad way . . .'

Jenny, who was standing next to John saw how pale and drawn he looked. 'Yes, it was pretty bad,' he whispered.

'Well, we were just about giving up hope,' continued Mr Miller, 'when we had a visitor.' Mr Miller paused, waiting to see their reaction.

'The Prince,' said Mrs Miller, softly, 'wasn't it?'

Mr Miller turned to her in pleased surprise. 'How did you know that?'

'Is he still here?' burst out Jenny in excitement.

Her face dropped as Mr Miller replied, 'No. He's gone.' He went on to tell them how the appearance of the Prince had paralysed Lasky and the other Grey Gunners, who were questioning them.

Mr Miller said he could not tell them exactly what the Prince had said to him—not yet anyway. But he had given him a message for Simon and Jenny that he would see them soon.

The Companions, who had gone in search of the Grey Gunners, had been surprised to find them paralysed and John and Mr Miller free. Lasky and the other Grey Gunners had been rounded up in the Treatment Room. They were there now, with the two remaining Companions on guard.

'Alexon,' said Michael, turning to the Companion who seemed to be the next in command, 'take them all to the ship and question them. I'll come as soon as I can.'

That was the last Simon and Jenny were to see of Grendra. But, at that moment, watching him being marched up the stairs to the Treatment Room, Simon felt that he would be sure to turn up again soon.

Jenny exclaimed in delight at the beauty of their surroundings as they walked out into the late morning sunshine. It was difficult to imagine that they had escaped so narrowly from such great danger, as they strolled down the drive, past flower-beds ablaze with colour.

'Where are we going now?' asked Simon. He and John were walking along on either side of Michael, with Mr and Mrs Miller deep in conversation just behind and Andromeda and Jenny with Alabaster last of all.

'Yes. Where are we going?' echoed Jenny brightly.

'Home,' replied Michael. 'All of us, in our different ways, are going home.'

'What do you mean?' asked Jenny slowly.

'Michael and I must return to the Star of the Prince, Jenny,' said Andromeda, slipping an arm round her shoulder.

'And we'll be able to finish our holiday,' said Mrs Miller happily. 'The whole family together and John,' she added, smiling at him.

Jenny stared blindly at the gravel path. Instead of the excitement of a few moments ago she now felt disappointed and cross. It was as if she had held in her hands the bright bubble of adventures to come, only to have it pricked with a few casual words.

Mr Miller and Michael were talking earnestly together before the Millers set off down the path towards the land-rover, with Simon and John following behind.

'We'll wait for you in the landrover, Jenny,' called her father.

Jenny slowly raised her eyes to find Andromeda watching her. She knew how badly she was behaving and made an effort to be cheerful.

'Here you are then, Andy,' she said brightly, handing over the sleeping ball of fur she was carrying. 'You can't go without Alabaster, can you?'

'Jenny,' said Andromeda as she took Alabaster carefully from her, 'it will be all right again soon. You must talk to the King about how you feel.'

Jenny looked at her bleakly, unable to say another word.

'This isn't really goodbye you know, Jenny,' Andromeda said with a reassuring smile.

'It isn't the end of the mission either,' added Michael. 'We want you to take this and give it to your mother and father. It holds the final clue.'

Jenny looked down at the ball of rainbow glass which Michael had placed in her hands.

'Remember, Jenny,' Michael added, 'you are not alone.'

She looked up, wanting to see the encouragement in his eyes which she had felt in his voice. But where Michael and Andromeda had been standing, there was only the early morning sunshine filtering through the trees.

'Not alone,' repeated Jenny in a whisper. She blinked back the tears which threatened to fall on to the rainbow ball.

She kept her eyes fixed on the ball as she walked slowly back to the landrover. As she looked the colours seemed to fuse for a moment, like a pattern in a kaleidoscope, so that words formed. The pattern shifted and a new set of words appeared. Jenny gazed at them, fascinated. Then suddenly the thought came that whatever clue was hidden in the rainbow ball, it was not for her.

'Give this to your mother and father,' Michael had said. She began to hurry back to the landrover, not bothering now to check the flow of angry tears. It was not her message, not her mission. The rainbow ball seemed to burn in her hands. She only wanted to be rid of it now.

The welcoming smile on her mother's face faded quickly as she saw Jenny's expression.

'Here, this is for you,' Jenny said indifferently, holding out the rainbow ball. 'Michael asked me to give it to you and Dad. It holds the last clue.'

Simon was both anxious and puzzled as he looked at the rainbow ball and then at Jenny. As she attempted to thrust the ball into their mother's hands he realised what was going to happen and leapt forward. But he was too late. As Mrs Miller hesitantly held out her hands, Jenny let go of the ball abruptly. It fell to the floor of the landrover and smashed into pieces. The rainbow ball was broken beyond repair and with it was gone the last clue and, it seemed, all hope of completing the mission.

# 14

The first week of the holiday was a miserable one. Jenny seemed to have withdrawn into herself and nothing any of them could say made any difference. By the end of the week her gloom seemed to be rubbing off on to Simon, so John suggested that the two of them get away into the heart of the conservation zone and go fishing.

Part of the reason Simon felt so fed up was that although he and John had talked to the King about how bad things were at the moment, nothing had happened. He almost wished they were back at the farm trying to escape from the Grey Gunners or fighting the Old Ruler. At least they had felt the power of the King on their side then. He felt worse when he remembered how excited they had felt once about coming home to tell people what the Prince had done for them and to share his power with them. What could he tell people now, when it seemed the power of the Prince was not even great enough to help Jenny?

'Looks like the Old Ruler has won after all,' he muttered to himself.

'Looks like you're not going to complete your mission,' commented John wryly. 'Come on, Simon. You don't mean that. Don't give up now!'

Simon concentrated on his fishing line and the calm surface of the river. 'The last clue is lost,' he said flatly, 'and Jenny just doesn't care any more. What can I do?'

'Be ready,' replied John.

Simon gave him a sidelong glance and turned back to his fishing line.

'Be ready to follow the Prince when he gives the signal,'

John went on. 'Remember that the King has put all power in the hands of the Prince. That means the Old Ruler doesn't really stand a chance. After all that's happened you should know that however black things look, the King has a plan.'

'And we just have to keep trusting him,' added Simon, with a tentative grin. As John had been talking Simon's heart had begun to lift. Suddenly he felt sure what they should do next. 'John, let's talk to the King again. Let's ask him to help Jenny feel excited and, this time, let's ask him to give us a second chance at that last clue.'

They felt it was a step forward when Jenny agreed to come and sit in the garden with them the following afternoon. She wouldn't join in their game of hand ball but at least she didn't want to hide away by herself.

Hot and thirsty from their game, the boys made their way across the lawn to the garden chairs where Jenny was sitting. Simon, heading for the lemonade on the table behind Jenny, playfully lobbed the ball at her as he passed her chair.

'Here, Jen, catch. Want some lemonade?'

Jenny had caught the ball neatly and was holding it in her hands, staring at it when Simon brought her lemonade.

'Feet that will walk back along the old path,' she said, 'and eyes that will see.'

She suddenly jumped up from the chair.

'I've remembered it! I've remembered a bit of the clue. There were words inside the rainbow ball. Where's Mum? I must tell her.' Without waiting for an answer, Jenny dashed inside the house, leaving the boys to follow.

But what Jenny remembered didn't really make any sense. Hard as she tried she simply could not remember any more. Fragments of words floated in front of her, but the harder she concentrated the quicker they slipped away.

As she watched her daughter scribbling down words on scraps of paper, frowning with concentration, Mrs Miller felt more and more anxious. It had been such a relief to see Jenny more like her old self, she was afraid that if Jenny couldn't remember the clue soon, she would sink back into the old misery again.

'Jenny,' she began, sitting down at the table with coffee and biscuits, 'why don't you go out for a day—blow the cobwebs away. You've hardly seen anything of the conservation zone this holiday and you know how much you love it. Getting away from everything may help you to think more clearly too. Why don't you go to Warwick-on-Arden tomorrow?'

Mr Miller had initiated an investigation through the Defence Plant and was certain that the Grey Gunners had left the conservation zone. They had obviously gone underground and it seemed most likely that they would reappear in different zones throughout the entire planet, but out of uniform.

So Jenny felt perfectly safe as she walked the old streets of Warwick-on-Arden, with its timbered houses and country gardens. It was like stepping back into another world centuries ago. The sun shone warmly on the old paving stones and the bright colours of the scented flowers gave Jenny such a feeling of well-being that she didn't even give a thought to the clue. As she set out for home, she felt happy and relaxed, and very hopeful that everything would turn out all right after all.

It was while she was away that Mr Miller had his brainwave. He had been out to the Defence Plant, and came bursting into the kitchen at lunch-time. Mrs Miller turned from putting a casserole into the old-style electric cooker.

'Mary! Where's Simon? I've got an idea. I can't imagine why we haven't thought of it before. Where's the code card Simon had?'

'Dad,' said Simon with exaggerated patience, 'it's no use looking at the code card. That was for the first part of the mission till we found you and Mum.'

'Besides,' added John, 'this is a new clue and it was in the rainbow ball.'

'Surely Andromeda would have said if the clue was on the code card as well,' Mrs Miller joined in. 'Why bother giving us the ball in the first place and why let Jenny go through all this misery after breaking it?'

Mr Miller was beginning to lose patience with them. 'What if I tell you that I think it's an idea the King has given me?' he said finally.

There was no more arguing. Simon went and fetched his code card immediately. Their excitement was quickly deflated when they discovered that they could do nothing to decode the clue. Jenny had hidden the decoding card, as they had agreed, in a safe place known only to her. They would have to wait until she arrived home.

The journey home for Jenny was partly on bicycle and partly on an old-fashioned train, which was much more fun than the present day inter-city speeders. As she looked out at the countryside Jenny began to think once more about the last clue and she did something which she had not done properly since Andromeda and Michael had left; she talked to the King.

There were a few people in the same carriage so she talked quietly under her breath. 'First of all, thank you for a lovely day. Thank you that the conservation zone is so beautiful.' She paused, uncertain how to phrase what she wanted to say next. 'I'm sorry I've behaved so badly. You probably know that I've thought things haven't been fair. I thought that perhaps we were going to meet the Prince and he was going to say "Well done, Simon and Jenny," or something like that and perhaps there would have been a party to celebrate. You know the rest too, how I felt that

Simon and I wouldn't have anything exciting to do any more and . . .' She let the tears trickle down her cheeks as the train plunged into a tunnel. 'I'm afraid that maybe I dropped the rainbow ball on purpose,' she finished on a sob. 'I really am sorry.' There was no more to say. But as she sat in the dimmed light she felt as if a great weight had been lifted from her.

Then the train rattled out of the tunnel into the mellow sunshine of early evening. At first Jenny was dazzled by the light and then afterwards she was never really sure exactly what she had seen. She felt that there was someone sitting next to her. Michael's words 'You are not alone,' came back to her as clearly as if someone had spoken them. She turned quickly, but the fleeting impression of a smiling face melted into the sunlight. Instead, in a pool of golden light on the worn seat was a small, purring bundle.

'Alabaster! Where did you come from?' exclaimed Jenny in delight. 'Thank you,' she added softly, fixing her eyes on the spot where, a few seconds before, she thought she had seen the face of the Prince.

So Jenny arrived home, bursting with the news of what had just happened. The rest of the family, eager to tell her about the last clue, all talked at once and gave Alabaster an enthusiastic welcome.

It was in a very excited mood that they finally tackled the code. The clue was obviously, from the bits Jenny remembered, the same clue that was in the rainbow ball. They could only suppose that the ball had been given specially to Jenny to help her hand over the leadership of the mission to her parents. Jenny told them about her experience on the train and repeated how sorry she was about the way she had behaved.

It was hard for any of them to be serious for long. There was great excitement as Mr Miller read out the completed clue.

*Feet that will travel an old path again*
*And eyes that will suddenly see;*
*Lips that will tell and hearts that will feel;*
*The new thing will grow when the old pain will heal;*
*All comes together when the breaking begins.*
*Understand this and men will be free.*

'Feet that will travel an old path again,' began Simon, 'is us coming back to where we started.'

'And eyes that will suddenly see,' continued Mr Miller, 'is us understanding this last bit of the mission.'

'I don't follow the next bit though,' frowned Mrs Miller.

'But,' Jenny said quietly, 'the next two bits apply to me; the old pain healing and the breaking beginning. I had to feel sorry about the way I've been behaving before we could begin to make sense of this clue.'

'You're right, darling,' said Mrs Miller, hugging her. 'How strange that this clue should be on the code card before the rainbow ball and everything else happened.'

'If you look at the last line, the third line begins to make sense,' exclaimed John. 'Men will be free, as the King means them to be, when we understand our mission. When we tell them!'

'Yes "Lips that will tell". Us again,' said Jenny, nodding, 'but what about "hearts that will feel"?'

'Us loving the people we share the good news with,' added Mrs Miller, smiling.

'So the mission is far from being over,' sighed Jenny happily.

'My goodness me, looks like it's only just beginning,' laughed Mr Miller.

'We've a lot of people to tell,' said John thoughtfully.

'But what a story we've got to tell them!' enthused Simon.

They all laughed. Then Jenny said quietly, 'I wish everyone knew the Prince like we do.'

'Tomorrow we'll start a plan of campaign,' said Mr Miller.

'Good gracious! It nearly is tomorrow!' exclaimed Mrs Miller looking at the kitchen clock.

'Hey, Mum,' suggested Simon, 'how about a midnight feast to celebrate?'

'Oh yes,' cried Jenny. 'Please?'

Mrs Miller looked round at the excited faces. There wouldn't be much sleeping done that night. 'Why not!' she agreed, smiling. 'What shall we have? Something to remember the adventure by.' She thought back to the farmhouse. 'How about bacon and eggs?'

'And ice-cream,' added Simon, hopefully.

'And chocolate biscuits,' chimed in Jenny, licking her lips.

'Not forgetting something special for Alabaster,' concluded Mrs Miller laughing.

'Miaow,' said Alabaster and, rubbing himself against her legs, purred with contentment.